Also by John Puddefoot

Logic and Affirmation (Scottish Academic Press 1987)
God and the Mind Machine (SPCK 1996)

WHAT ABOUT CHRISTIANITY?

Answers for the Modern World

John Puddefoot

SPCK

First published in Great Britain 1997
Society for Promoting Christian Knowledge
Holy Trinity Church
Marylebone Road
London
NW1 4DU

British Library Cataloguing-in-Publication Data

A catalogue record for this book is available from the British Library

ISBN 0-281-05041-4

Typeset by Wilmaset Ltd, Wirral
Printed in Great Britain by
Biddles Ltd, Guildford and King's Lynn

CONTENTS

Preface	vii
Foreword by Richard Holloway	xi
What about Somewhere to Start?	1
What about Science?	6
What about Wishful Thinking?	7
What about Truth?	9
What about Belief?	10
What about Salvation?	12
What about Other Religions?	14
What about Heaven?	15
What about Hell?	16
What about Tradition?	17
What about Authority?	18
What about the Bible?	21
What about Inspiration?	22
What about the Word become Flesh?	24
What about Grace?	26
What about Conversion?	30
What about Me?	32
What about Jesus?	35
What about Fundamentalism?	36
What about Worship?	38
What about God the Father?	41
What about the Crucifixion?	43
What about Presence?	46
What about Transformation?	48
What about Ministry?	50

What about God? 52
What about Suffering? 57
What about Death? 59
What about Evolution? 61
What about Jesus (Again)? 63
What about Creation? 64
What about the Trinity? 65
What about the Holy Spirit? 67
What about Freedom? 69
What about Morality? 70
What about Consistency? 72
What about Doctrine? 75
What about the Church? 77
What about Prayer? 78
What about Revelation? 84
What about Spirituality? 85
What about Christianity? 99

Foreword by Richard Holloway

Words are funny things, more complicated than we often realize. The words themselves may be the same throughout the generations, but their meanings change, sometimes radically. This is certainly true of religious words and it is why Christianity is committed to a permanent task of interpretation, of finding new meanings in old words. If we ignore this duty of interpretation, people reject faith for the wrong reasons. If the old meaning of words such as 'God', 'Jesus', 'salvation' and 'worship' do not make sense to us, we may reject them completely and lose touch with the hidden, precious realities they refer to. When we are asked about Christianity we are likely to dismiss it as an outworn creed, with no relevance for us today. But, 'What about Christianity?' Can it bear any meaning for us today? This stimulating book addresses this question. It wants us to find today's meaning in the old religious words.

What are we doing, anyway, when we talk about religion? Are we talking about something out there or only about something in here? Normally, when we use language we expect it to refer to something out there. The word 'cow', for example, refers to a four-legged animal with a bulging udder that stands around in fields eating grass. It is true that we might have come up with a different word by which to refer to the cow, such as 'pid'. The creature would be the same, though the vocal symbol we used to refer to it would be different. Whenever we heard or read the word 'pid', however, we would visualize the creature we now think of as a cow. One of the interesting things about learning a new language is the way it gives us different ways of referring to familiar objects. It is obvious, therefore, that there is something arbitrary about language. It is clearly essential to us if we are to communicate to and with each other, but the symbols we use, the things we call words, especially when they are nouns that name things, could be any set of sounds we care to choose. In some languages, such as the ones used by certain of the Native

American communities in North America, it is believed that there is a living, almost mystical connection between word and that to which it refers. There are, for instance, a number of words that refer to the sound made by the wind blowing through the leaves of a tree; the words themselves suggest as well as refer to the sound. However, this kind of verbal mysticism does not break the main rule of language, which is that, to have meaning, it must refer to something beyond itself. Of course, we can play with language in all sorts of ways. Poets use language to suggest the reality they are referring to. At its best, poetry achieves an immediacy of experience that allows us to enter the reality to which the words refer. The power of poetry to move us lies in this mystery of immediacy. Poets of genius do not tell us about something; by their use of language they enable us to experience it for ourselves. George Steiner calls this the experience of *the real presence*, something transcendent enters the language and communicates itself to us directly. This means that language is sometimes more than itself and can be used as a means of revelation, as a way of encounter with something we had not previously known.

But what about religious language? Is it about anything out there, or is it always about our own reality, always about the human experience? The tough, modern answer to that question is that religious language is always and only a way of talking about our experiences of ourselves. After all, we only know the world and our own reality, so the vocal symbols we use can only refer to what we know. This is why some theologians say that the word 'God' does not refer to anything beyond the use we make of it – there is nothing out there to which it refers. We can go on using the word if we want too, as long as we realize that it is only the shorthand term for our own best values and longings.

The opposite of this reductive use of religious language is the point of view that treats words about God and faith as though they were themselves sacred, almost divine. We see this approach at its strongest in certain kinds of theories of Scripture that treat the words as if they were equivalent to the things to which they refer. They are no longer thought of as symbolic, signs that point away from themselves to some other reality to which they refer, but as substantive realities in themselves. People who believe in this approach call themselves literalists: the sacred words have to be believed in, not just the mysterious realities to which they point. It does not matter if we believe that this is a fundamental misunderstanding of language: the fact remains that there are lots of people who use religious language in this way.

So we seem to be caught between a rock and a hard place, between reductionists and literalists, between people who believe that religious words do not connect us with anything outside our own heads and people who believe that the words themselves are quasi-divine and can only be understood in the way they understand them.

Can nothing rescue us from this futile stand-off? In this book, John Puddefoot shows us one way of escaping from this stultifying dilemma. He is not a reductionist: he believes that religious language is about more than noises in our own heads – like the best poetry, it can put us in touch with mysteries that call out to us. But the words themselves are symbolic, they point away from themselves, so we are not to be obsessed with them, too dependent upon any one way of interpreting them. In this book he takes a refreshingly new look at the old words and phrases and finds meaning in them that will be appropriate to us in our day. Paul Tillich once said that Jesus Christ had to be our contemporary if he was to have any meaning for us: the Jesus who was right for a first-century Jew or a tenth-century monk was not Jesus for us today. We cannot become chronological emigrants. Jesus, if he is real, must be encountered by us today. *What about Christianity?* confronts us with the meaning of Jesus Christ for us today.

Richard Holloway
Edinburgh

In memory
of my
Father,
Charles Gregory *Puddefoot,*
1912–1991
who taught me more about Christianity *than he knew*

Preface

How does the Church reach out to those who seldom darken its doors? To those with heart-felt questions which they feel they cannot voice or which, if voiced, receive no adequate answers? How, when human beings in crisis turn to drink or drugs, can we ask them this question: What about Christianity?

Many people groan at the thought of Christianity. They perceive it as out-of-date, a cosy club, a communion of fools, a pastime of those with nothing better to do. In three years roaming inhospitable factories as an industrial chaplain, and twelve more years facing the persistent questioning of adolescent boys as a teacher, I have come to the conclusion that we have to be honest about the problems Christianity faces and dare to voice radically new solutions.

This book asks simple, basic questions many people want to ask, but feel they dare not ask: What about Jesus? What about death? What about suffering? What about resurrection? What about just about everything Christianity stands for in a world that has lost touch with its language?

This is a book aimed beyond the boundaries of the Church at the no-man's-land of the questioning unbeliever, the agnostic, and anyone genuinely seeking a new, fresh approach to Christian truth. But it also aims to equip churchpeople with a new armoury of responses to antagonistic questions to which they often have no adequate answers. It is a missionary book which is prepared to go more than halfway to meet sceptics on their own ground. It strives to explore their questions with a soul-searching determination to root out nonsense, however ruthless the resulting answers may seem. It aims to be a tough, honest, no-holds-barred exploration of Christianity from a point of view that many will share, most will respect, but some will deplore.

My thanks go to Richard Holloway for his thoughtful and stimulating foreword, to the staff of SPCK for their professionalism, patience and help, and to my family for the kinds of things families should be thanked for, not least their tolerance of neglect.

What about Somewhere to Start?

Where religion is concerned, most people today start with questions. The answers to those questions prompt more questions. 'Yes, but what about . . . ?'

This book takes these questions seriously. Belief should always take the questions of unbelief seriously. Yet, paradoxically, it often seems that the more fervently and passionately we profess to believe in the God who makes himself known in Jesus Christ, the less ready we become to identify with those who have the severest doubts and the most searching questions about our faith. It is as if, for all our protestations of belief, we are worried that we will be contaminated by their questions.

From my starting-point, this is a self-contradiction. To believe fervently and passionately in Jesus, however many defects there are in that belief, however many faults there are in the way we live out that belief in our lives, must be – or so it seems to me – to cease to worry about what will happen to us if we engage with unbelief. For what value or credibility does a belief have which is so frightened of the questions posed by unbelief that it would rather not face them? What credibility does a shepherd have who is more concerned for himself (or for the sheep safely in the fold) than for the lost sheep that remain out in the wilderness? Where in this is the 'faith beyond faith' that, even if we forget God, God will not forget us?

My own starting-point can therefore be put very simply. It follows directly from my experience of Jesus that I should take your doubts and questions more seriously than my own belief. Belief in Jesus has, as one of its first fruits, a complete loss of concern for the correctness of that same belief. Truly to experience the love of God in Jesus is to be persuaded that however well or however poorly I believe in him – however correctly or incorrectly as measured by the canons of Scripture and Christian tradition – really does not matter. What matters is that he believes in me. It is that belief, his belief – not my belief – that sets me free.

Any religion worth belonging to must be robust enough to respond positively to the most penetrating questions that can be asked of it and every member of that religion has a part to play in that response. Wherever a religion or its practitioners attempt to duck these questions, there we should be at our most suspicious. Faith must not be afraid of questions. Real faith thrives on them and is strengthened by them. And new questions demand new answers, even if many of those answers are reworked versions of much older answers. Questions are to be taken seriously.

However, questions need to be answered in ways which take account of the starting-point of the questioner. To answer a question in a way that fails to take that starting-point seriously is almost certainly to offer an answer which cannot be heard. Those not convinced by the Bible, the mainstream Christian doctrines, the worship-patterns of the churches, and with no personal experience of belief in Jesus, cannot 'hear' an answer couched in highly orthodox, conventional terms. They do not start from there.

Unfortunately, the answers Christians give are usually couched in exactly these conventional terms. It is assumed that Christian truth stands where it must stand and that anyone wishing to know more about it must understand it in its traditional form as expressed in traditional language. Either that, or it is presented in a way which insults the intelligence. But can accepting Christianity 'like a little child' really involve abandoning all our wit and intelligence and scepticism first? Is it not more that Jesus meant that we need to rediscover something of the wide-eyed wonder of childhood, of exuberance in the richness of life, rather than be willing to accept anything we are told and place ourselves at the mercy of every religious madman, eccentric and charlatan?

So taking today's questions seriously involves doing more than giving answers couched in traditional Christian language.

It involves taking some risks by daring to put old answers into new words and being ready to share sceptical questions by entering into the world in which they arise. It is no good answering someone who does not believe in the inerrancy of the Bible, the infallibility of the Church, the need for worship, the authority of Jesus, or even the existence of God, in ways which already presuppose one or more of those beliefs.

Even so, this openness must be more than a front, a kind of 'loss leader' which quickly dissolves into something we have heard in much the same words many times before. What is on offer in the end must be something genuinely fresh and revitalizing, not just a reworking of a religion that relies upon unquestioning acceptance of Bible, Church, Jesus and God. Having set foot upon the path of radical, soul-searching questions, we must be ready to pursue it wherever it leads, even if that involves challenging some of our more cherished Christian assumptions about the Bible, the tradition, worship, prayer and God.

If this approach succeeds, this book will appeal primarily to two kinds of people: Christians who genuinely want to share what they believe with others, but who find it well-nigh impossible to commend it in the form it now generally assumes across wide tracts of the western world; and non-Christians who genuinely want to understand what it is that Christianity really involves and who are searching for a deeper spiritual life, but who find the forms in which Christianity usually presents itself either impossible to accept, insulting to their intelligence, or dismissive of the heart-felt doubts they voice.

I am conscious that this approach most risks offending those for whom Christianity is a matter of 'take it or leave it', who see Christian truth as expressed in the Bible, the tradition, worship and prayer as too precious to be subjected to the kind of questioning that comes from the secular world. They are likely to believe that the world must first learn the language of Christianity in its traditional form and that Christianity has no responsibility to 'go the second mile' with those who tap hesitantly on its doors. The only justification for a fundamentally different approach – but the only justification we need – is the central Christian belief that Jesus 'humbled himself' (Philippians 2.8) for the same purpose.

Each of the answers given in this book is a record of one of my own answers to one of my own questions. There is no 'window-dressing' here. These are neither questions nor answers which I have dreamt up to try to sugar the pill of Christianity, or to lure the unsuspecting into a commitment to routine institutional religion. There is no 'So now you will start going to church, won't you?' at the end of this long and winding road. I have, in truth, only one motive: the hope that by facing my own questions and recording the answers which I have accepted, I may help others to find some new freshness in Christianity which will enable them to know God better through Jesus Christ in the power of the Holy Spirit. But to hope for that is also, in a sense, to hope for everything.

So I shall start with questions and I shall pursue the answers in the questions that will come later: 'Yes, but what about . . . ?'

Where do I start myself? I do believe in Jesus – fervently, passionately, completely, wholly – and badly. My belief, although I pay lip-service to it most of the time, comes and goes. I waver; I have doubts; I rebel; I argue. But at bottom I believe – fervently, passionately, completely, wholly.

What do I believe? That of all the human beings who have ever lived, if I were asked to pick one whom human beings should know, it would be Jesus. If you gave me the chance to meet any one person in all history, I would choose Jesus (but I would be rather nervous about what he might say to me and what I might find out about myself).

Why do I believe Jesus to be so important? Because I believe Jesus to be the best (and in many ways the only) way we come to know anything at all important about God. Here you will protest: but what about the idea that he was just a holy man, a prophet, a teacher; what about all we learn from the universe; what about nature; what about the Bible; what about the Church; what about . . . ? I acknowledge that all these other sources matter, but I do not think that they come anywhere near to being as important as Jesus himself. Jesus is important in a way that they are not because in Jesus we meet God as a human being. We know more about human beings than we know about anything else, and so in knowing Jesus we know more about God than by knowing anything else. And Jesus is an active partner in this relationship because he is real and alive (although I do not expect anyone to take my word for that).

But what about all the doubts we have about the Bible? How can we be sure that Jesus is not being lied about; how can we be sure that Jesus did not lie? How can we know that such things as the miracles or the resurrection happened at all?

The honest answer is that we cannot be sure about any of these things. Not if by 'sure' we mean 'in a way that could not possibly be wrong no matter how hard we tried to doubt it'. But all that we know is like that. I could be wrong that there is a table under my dinner plate, that this is a computer in front of me, that there are other people in the world. But we do not take such doubts seriously, largely because these are not isolated beliefs: they form part of a tapestry of interlocking beliefs about the world. Some of these beliefs may be wrong, but they cannot all be wrong in so serious a way as to make life impossible (since life is clearly not impossible, however difficult it may be).

It is the same with a religion or a person. Individual things may be doubtful, questionable, difficult to swallow, but we make up our minds about a total package of teachings and practices on the basis of its overall appeal. Sometimes we will be influenced to a considerable extent by a personal figure. In my experience – but that is not something I expect others to take seriously just because I say so – it is the person of Jesus who makes the difference. But I shall have to say a lot before that amounts to more than an affirmation of my own conviction. And, as I say, I do not expect my conviction to carry any weight with anyone else at all.

But at the outset there does seem to be a major obstacle to such a belief, especially to someone with a mathematical, scientific, rational frame of mind such as me.

What about Science?

Science seems at first sight to offer a strong alternative source of certainty. We know a lot about all sorts of things because of science, and it seems to be more or less foolproof. So many very clever people could not be completely wrong (even if they are wrong in a few details). And not all religious people claim to be as clever, so seem much more likely to be wrong. It does not seem to make sense to make stronger claims for what we know about Jesus than for what we know through science. Surely we must accept that science is more certain?

I do not think that we should accept anything of the sort. Science tells us a great deal that we should also believe. There are few mainstream scientific claims about which I, at least, have very serious doubts. Yet I simply do not understand arguments that seem to imply that the more I understand about the universe through science, the less I can or should need to believe in God. A similar sort of argument would imply that the more I knew about the workings of the human body, the less reason I would have to believe that there was a mind directing it. Yet even the most sceptical scientists do not draw this conclusion from advances in biology and medicine.

So science too is part of the world of beliefs I have that are centred on Jesus. Of course, I do not need Jesus to make scientific theories work, but nothing in science tells me anything that makes my belief in Jesus less likely to be true. Some scientist, of course, like to ridicule religion, and misrepresent it; but in any case their views as scientists do not make science itself contradict religion. There are far too many religious scientists for that to be true.

Some scientists (and also on occasion some Christians) like to try to explain things like the Virgin Birth, the resurrection or the miracles in terms of the laws of physics, chemistry and biology. For example, when the Turin Shroud was a major focus of interest and inspiration, many papers were written about how the image on the cloth might be the result of some form of radiation emitted as the body was resurrected. We should have viewed all this as complete nonsense. What happened in the resurrection had nothing to do with the laws of this universe. To claim otherwise is to misunderstand the kind of claim that is being made in the resurrection. The same kind of mistake turns God into something natural that we can explain using nature's laws.

We shall return to discuss scientific theories of creation and evolution later on. At the moment, we need to address a more immediate question. In view of the apparently all-encompassing power of science, is it not just perverse to persist with belief in God? Does not belief in God just reflect the wishful thinking of those who refuse to face reality?

What about Wishful Thinking?

The Virgin Birth is a good example of a place where science and religion collide and where wishful thinking seems to take over. Some would like to write it off as an early theological mistake based upon a misunderstanding of Isaiah 7.14. Others would dismiss the miracles as the products of stories that grew in the telling, or the resurrection as something merely psychological that the disciples invented to offset their grief at Jesus' horrific death. The sceptics think that believing anything else is just wishful thinking, especially believing that Jesus was really God in human form. They read such wishful thinking as a product of gullibility or personal inadequacy: grown men and women just do not believe such things any more.

There is, of course, no hard evidence to support any of these things. The Bible, for example, once we realize that it may, like any human story-telling, embellish the truth, becomes a source of potentially endless misrepresentations and embellishments. We almost certainly end up, if we choose to be sceptical, with a set of beliefs that have been invented and then grown in the telling.

But it is possible to see things differently. It is possible that all or many of these things actually happened. And even if they did not quite happen as the Bible says, that does not mean that they did not happen at all, or that the way the Bible tells us about them lacks any value. The Bible need not be (and I think cannot be) either wholly true or wholly false. Only our wishful thinking makes it seem one or the other. Making religion complete nonsense may be the product of wishful thinking too. The virgin birth, the miracles and the resurrection are not impossible. At least, not if we believe in a real God who really does control the whole universe. But we are increasingly embarrassed to admit that we believe any such thing.

So why do I believe all these things? I am going to give an answer which may look like exactly the kind of wishful thinking I am talking about in this section, but is actually much more than that. It is certainly not the kind of answer you might expect: no Damascus Road experience that changed my life; no seeing of visions nor dreaming of dreams; no belief in the infallibility of Bible, Church or tradition; no claim to have a hot-line to God.

I believe these things because taken together and as part of a complete set of beliefs they make life more interesting and complete than if I do not believe them.

Now that sounds exactly like wishful thinking. It sounds as if it would be a reason to believe in all sorts of other things that I actually do not believe in (ghosts, UFOs, aliens landing from other worlds, astrology, fortune telling, and so on). And it could be such a reason. But the difference is that I actually do *not* believe in these other things because I do not think that they make life more interesting. I think they make life rather silly. They are, in that sense, irrational.

What about Truth?

I believe in God, Jesus, the Holy Spirit, the Virgin Birth, miracles and the resurrection because my life, my whole being, echoes and resonates to the whole system of ideas from which they come in a way that makes me feel more alive.

The sceptic and the cynic will say, 'So what!' or, 'What's that got to do with whether they are true?' And to them I would answer that it has everything to do with whether they are true because (although most of us probably do not realize it) we actually use this approach to decide whether anything at all we could believe is true.

These ideas are not true because I believe them (that would be a foolish thing to say). I rather see the fact that they make my whole life richer, and my whole being more resonant, as the best clue to their truth I could possibly have. In fact I see it as the only clue to the truth of anything that anybody can possibly have. We decide whether things are true by assessing the effect they have upon us: if they feel right (in this really deep sort of sense), we believe; if they don't, we don't believe. True beliefs move us and change us.

Of course we like to think that we have much better, more reliable ways to decide whether things are true. We have theories and experiments and reason and long experience. But what does each of these depend upon? Theories are based upon assumptions we make which we believe to be true, and we believe them to be true because they feel right. The scientific community as a whole finds itself excited by these assumptions because they resonate with their theories. Experiments depend upon skill and feel for reliable results; those results depend upon beliefs about the way the experiments have been conducted, and we judge those by whether they feel right. Reason relies upon our ability to recognize a good, convincing argument when we see one or hear one. But we cannot check every single statement in an argument, tracing it back through the centuries to some early single absolute truth, so we rely in the end on whether we are persuaded, and we judge whether to be persuaded by whether the conclusions feel right to us, which is to say whether they resonate inside us. And long experience is needed to decide upon whether we feel we can trust the things others tell us they have seen, felt, touched, and so forth (even scientists); and that trust in what they say is based upon whether we feel those who speak to be trustworthy.

So in the end our ability to assess truth boils down to our ability to detect the right sorts of resonances inside ourselves, and those resonances are linked tightly to the ability to decide to whom we should listen and which influences we should allow to impinge upon our lives. We will accept what feels right; we will reject what feels wrong.

Of course, lots of things come to us in wrappings which hide their dependence on feelings. Most of science and mathematics is hard to accept or reject piece-by-piece; we either take it all or none of it. Some reject it all, not by denying that it is true, but simply by refusing to have anything to do with it. They live their lives entirely differently, in different worlds. Equally, some scientists have little or no interest in philosophy, religion, literature or art. They do not resonate for them.

So the first thing I have to say about belief in my quest for new answers to old questions is that I believe things because they make like more interesting and complete, because they allow my body to echo with resonant 'sounds' which make me more alive. But there is a second, and perhaps more far-reaching, thing I want to say about belief.

What about Belief?

It does not actually matter whether these indifferent scientists and other atheists and agnostics believe in God, Jesus and the whole system we call Christianity or not insofar as beliefs involve statements of doctrine. To think that it does matter in this way is to have made a basic mistake about the nature and importance of belief.

Those who have been led to believe that without belief in Jesus we cannot be saved may be shocked by this, because to say that it does not matter whether people believe in Jesus or not seems like saying it does not matter whether they are saved or not.

Of course it matters. But what does it mean to be saved? And what is the connection between being saved and believing in Jesus?

I actually thing that the important word here is not 'believe' but 'in'. We know what belief is, but what is belief 'in' something? For long centuries we have tended to say that belief in Jesus boils down to being ready to say that we agree with certain lists of teachings or doctrines (such as we find in the creeds). So believing in Jesus becomes the same thing as saying 'I believe in God' and 'I believe in the creation of the world by God' and all the other things Christians say they believe. But this sort of belief is of no importance, or at least of no more importance than saying 'I believe in football' or 'I believe Wellington won the battle of Waterloo' or 'I believe that two plus two equals four'.

No, belief 'in' Jesus is about living life 'in' Jesus. It is about finding a way to live in which what we say and do and what Jesus says and does are somehow linked together. 'Whoever believes in him shall not perish but have eternal life' (John 3.16) really must not be understood as if it amounted to saying what the Athanasian Creed says (which has nothing to do with Athanasius, incidentally), 'Whosoever will be saved ... it is necessary that he hold the Catholic Faith. Which Faith except every one do keep whole and undefiled, without doubt he shall perish everlastingly.' This just doesn't mean anything as far as I can see. It seems to suggest that mouthing certain teachings and doctrines will 'save us' whether they make any sense or any difference to us or not. Salvation becomes a matter of passing some kind of cosmic multiple-choice examination.

'Believing in Jesus' in this sense does nobody any good. This kind of salvation is no kind of salvation at all.

What about Salvation?

Salvation is not about ticking boxes next to doctrines we do not understand. It is about becoming a new person 'in' Jesus. It is about changing and being changed, being converted to a new way of life, sharing in the glory that comes to us when our whole being resonates to the truth which is found only in God.

That I scarcely ever think about salvation – especially my own – probably says as much about my theology as any other single observation could. Yet salvation is a central theme in Christianity, and in some respects what the whole edifice stands or falls by. But questions abound as soon as we start: Is salvation individual, communal or global? Does the universe require salvation, or only its inhabitants? Are we being saved *from* something or *for* something or both or neither? What, if anything, are we being saved from or for?

A conventional, traditional answer, would identify salvation as that process by which God cleanses us of guilt and culpability for our sin. And our sin would be seen not in terms of the multitude of sins we commit, but in terms of the state in which we exist. The death of Christ would, in many such accounts, be seen in terms of the sacrificial lamb slaughtered to remove the guilt of the world, and as an offering to God.

But most modern minds find the notion of a God who requires a blood-sacrifice to turn aside his wrath difficult or impossible to accept. And those same modern minds find it difficult to understand what, if anything, could be meant by the sin of the world or the corruption of the universe, the cosmic fall from grace or the guilt that accompanies birth into the world through Original Sin. Such minds are deeply, perhaps fatally perplexed. It is as if a language is being spoken that employs a vocabulary that is alien and a set of concepts which are unintelligible.

Small wonder that for many the concept of salvation has been altered and either made into a matter of individual redemption, the salvation of 'my' soul from the guilt of sin, or made into a matter of social and political justice. 'Are you saved, brother?' is the individualized version; somehow salvation becomes a matter of 'my' salvation and whether 'I' am inside or outside some sort of apparently exclusive club.

Salvation scarcely ever enters into my own thinking because I find all three of these accounts of what it might mean either offensive (as in the first) or trivial (as in both the alternatives). A notion of Jesus Christ's life and death that reduces him merely to the status of moral exemplar, spiritual guru, socio-political activist, or individual martyr, is not a reason for being a Christian or for regarding Jesus as in any sense a central figure in one's life.

Instead I find myself wanting to advocate a fourth, rather old-fashioned, way which will be felt by many to be even more obscure and incomprehensible than the other three. What Jesus saves us from (and, although we tend not to notice this) saves God from, is an everlasting separation between who God is and who we are. The injustice of a God who recommends pain, suffering and death for other people (because it is a necessary part of evolution and growth) is so great that only an incarnate God is exonerated from guilt for it. 'If life is so good, then how come you're not sharing it with us?' would otherwise be a perfectly proper, if disrespectful retort.

And yet this is my salvation, our salvation, and the world's salvation: that however miserable or pointless our lot may seem, however much it might seem to justify despair and even suicide, God in the Word made flesh in Jesus Christ experienced the same kind of degradation, humiliation, foresakenness, solitude, pain, sorrow, meaninglessness and death – and maybe even the same self-pity – that accompanies each of us down life's long, winding and sometimes bloody road.

This life justifies God for having created all life, all lives, all worlds, all galaxies. In this life the gulf that separates what it is like to be God and what it is like to be a human being is bridged and closed. In this life, for all the emptiness and meaninglessness of its lonely, painful death, we see God affirming that whatever may befall us, the chance of life is better than no chance at all. And if that is not the good news of our salvation, what is?

And that means something else that is important. Belief in Jesus does not lead us to salvation somewhere later in life, 'down the line', when we are offered the reward for what we have agreed to believe (almost like a gold star awarded by a divine teacher for those who have done well in a test). No, belief in Jesus means that our salvation is already upon us, already here, already changing our lives. It is its own, immediate reward. 'The kingdom of heaven is at hand.' We can begin to enjoy the glory of God we find in Jesus today, as our whole being resonates to the Jesus who is God's glory.

What about Other Religions?

Of course, all this makes it sound as if only Christians are saved. And in a sense that is true in that only Christians (by definition) believe in Jesus and share the vision of the glory of God that comes from that belief. That vision is their salvation, so we cannot talk about members of other religions being 'saved' in quite the same way.

But we must not confuse 'being saved' with things like going to heaven and going to hell. We must not be tempted to write off other religions because they do not believe in Jesus. If belief in Jesus is its own reward, and if the vision of the glory of God that makes our lives more interesting, more full, more joyful comes with that belief, saying that members of other religions (and of none) are not saved simply means they do not share the same vision of God's glory.

But there is no reason to say that they do not share some other kind of vision, or that those who share that vision are inferior. There is just no point in saying that. Those who enjoy a vision of God in their own lives will not want to dismiss those who do not as their inferiors, because the nature of that joy is that others are the poorer for the lack of it.

What about Heaven?

Will members of other religions go to heaven? The honest answer is, 'Who can say whether a Christian will go to heaven?' and an even more honest one is, 'Should such a question matter?'

Once we start to want to separate those who are going to heaven from those who are not (and many many Christians have wanted to do that for many reasons down the centuries, often with tragic consequences), we are tacitly denying that belief in Jesus is its own reward. Heaven we see as the final bonus on our insurance policy, something we have saved for and which is not to be given to others. Jesus showed the folly of this with the parable of the labourers in the vineyard (Matthew 20.1–16), which applies even and perhaps especially to lifelong believers. There is no good reason to think of everlasting life as a reward for earthly belief, and there are very good reasons to think another way.

To have experienced the fullness of being that comes from a vision of God based upon Jesus is automatically to want others to share in that vision. Any suggestion that we might obtain any satisfaction from the idea that others who have been denied this joy in their earthly lives might also be denied it in their heavenly lives (by being denied a heavenly life and/or consigned to hell) contradicts the basic vision itself: to experience something that good is to want everyone to share it. To claim a vision of the glory of God which makes us feel pleased when others reject it or do not enjoy it too, is to claim to experience something that is self-contradictory or that points the finger at the selfishness of so many of our religious attitudes.

Exactly the same kind of mistake arises when we see everlasting life in heaven with God as some kind of reward for our earthly belief (perhaps even our earthly worship, for much worship is so unworthy a reflection of the vision of glory I have been describing that the only conceivable reason to continue to share in it is that you hope it will earn you a compensating reward later).

In fact, the notion that we will earn a reward for our beliefs is also tied up with the fact that we lack any coherent reason for believing many of the things we believe other than that we think God wants us to believe them (because one of the churches tells us so). My reward for believing all these incomprehensible and occasionally ludicrous things, in other words, is that I shall be given a place in heaven for my selfless commitment to a whole list of things I do not begin to understand.

What about Hell?

Another reason we hope for a reward is that we think it very unjust that good people go unrewarded or that evil people go unpunished. If we have set aside the idea of hell, it seems that evil people get clean away with their evil, and that there is no justice.

But again the notion of punishment and reward has been distorted. If the vision of God's glory is its own reward, those who lack it are already living diminished lives, and that is itself a punishment. They may in the course of those lives inflict ghastly suffering on other human beings and animals, but what more pressing demonstration of their evil could there be than for them to be shown the error of their ways? Show evil people how evil they have been and they will punish themselves.

Do we really want to dispense with hell? Certainly, if hell is envisaged as a place of fire and torture, for the logic of the argument we have just worked through is that hell is a state of grace before God in full knowledge of one's earthly sin. That is the logic of God's glory, that those who see it are automatically convicted of their sin, and some no doubt will be unable to live with that knowledge, and will depart from God's presence to hide in everlasting shadow and shame merely to avoid seeing their own sinfulness as illuminated by his own all-seeing light.

But doesn't all this fly in the face of the teaching of Jesus in the New Testament? On many occasions he speaks of dividing sheep from goats (Matthew 25.32–33), wheat from chaff (Matthew 3.12), and he warns those who opposed him of the dangers of hell fire (Mark 9.47). And the Old Testament is constantly speaking of reward and punishment, God's wrath directed against Israel and the other nations who oppose his will and persecute his chosen people.

Are we not being rather cavalier in rewriting this evidence? Surely we have to contend with the whole history of Christian thought in order to rearrange the system of beliefs in the way that is being suggested here? Perhaps so, but there does seem to be a fundamental and inescapable contradiction between claiming, on the one hand, that my life has been changed by the discovery of the forgiving love of God made known in Jesus, and on the other being perfectly content to consign the whole of non-Christian humanity to everlasting fire and damnation.

What about Tradition?

But what about the two-thousand-year history of teaching and thought and prayer in the Church? Most of that remained faithful to the New Testament view of Jesus' teaching and warned all human beings of the dangers of being inside and outside the ark of salvation. Men and women were burned because they doubted the historic teaching of the Church, and countless millions have been satisfied to believe what the Church teaches, do what the Church commands, and to trust in God that they will therefore receive their reward in heaven. On what basis can we overturn such a long and distinguished history of faith and practice?

Do we have the right to set our own beliefs over against the Bible and the traditions of the Church? I want to turn the question round: what kind of a person is it who mindlessly repeats and passes on beliefs and practices which have led human beings to burn one another on points of doctrine, to wage war over the minutiae of scriptural interpretation, and to be set at one another's throats for centuries like Swift's Big-endians and Little-endians in *Gulliver's Travels*? What kind of a right is asserted, in other words, which is exercised in the face of all sense of proportion at the expense of incalculable inhumanity to other human beings? Slavish adherence to tradition and to the prevailing practices of a society or culture condemns us to the morality of the gas chamber, a morality which is no morality at all.

That seems to imply that authority lies ultimately inside ourselves, rather than in the Church or the Bible. Can this be so?

What about Authority?

Whatever evidence we have – from the Bible, from the Church, from other ancient documents, from very limited archaeological sources, and even from the climate of opinion in our own time and place – we cannot escape from or set aside the need to make up our own minds. For suppose we had been raised to believe in witches, fairies and black magic. We might well find ourselves in a family and belonging to a section of society whose beliefs (from a Christian point of view) are silly, dangerous and even evil. An argument from tradition and practice would allow believers in witches and these other things to remain faithful to them. An argument from tradition and practice would have prevented Jesus' disciples from 'leaving their nets'.

Now it is also true – and it is important not to avoid this admission – that someone could remain true to, say, beliefs in witches, after making up his or her own mind on the basis of what I am calling resonance, deep feelings of unity and fullness of life. But it is part of my faith that whatever resonances are available to us about, say, witches, pale into insignificance when compared with the resonances available through genuine encounter with the set of beliefs of God in Jesus that I am attempting to approach from a new angle here. If I did not believe that, I might become a believer in witches as well. And because of the radical change which Jesus made possible in the lives of his disciples, because of the way he gave them permission to question the prevailing traditions and practices of their time, I feel that each of us is also empowered by Jesus to take a fresh look at belief and to ask for ourselves, 'What about Christianity?'

But I also believe that genuinely worthwhile beliefs are their own reward in that they open our minds to possibilities we might otherwise never consider. A belief which only offers us hope of reward later (as if, with the White Queen from *Through the Looking-Glass*, Christianity involved habitually believing six impossible things before breakfast) is not worth holding. It may offer us hope of increasing reward as we grow more familiar with all its nooks and crannies, but it does not suggest that we should be prepared to put up with empty practices and beliefs that make no sense now for the sake of something as vague as everlasting life in heaven.

Therefore, on the basis of my own authority, if I find it impossible to endorse a belief because it strikes me as meaningless or absurd, I have (after a suitable amount of thought and careful consideration) several choices: to reject it (even if that seems to contradict the Bible or the tradition of the Church); to accept it reluctantly despite the fact that it makes no sense to me (because I believe that neither Bible nor Church tradition can be that wrong); or to place it in a kind of limbo, refusing to accept it myself at the present, but allowing for the possibility that my attitude may change later on (as I mature in the faith and my vision of God's glory grows). These are not trivial decisions, because the beliefs which I hold – if they are to be worth holding at all – I hold so strongly that they help to define the kind of human being I am. And to hold a belief that I find meaningless just because someone tells me that I should (for the sake of my immortal soul, let us say, or perhaps, more realistically, as at some periods in history, for fear of what the Church might do to me otherwise), offends against the principle that I must take responsibility for the kind of person that I am and that I shall one day become. And to counterbalance that insistence – for example to persuade me to hold on to a belief sufficiently long to understand what it may mean and how much it may enrich my life – requires the Church to possess a day-to-day credibility of the highest order. I very much doubt that any of today's churches have that authority.

If this seems a revolutionary suggestion, perhaps something that amounts to inciting believers to reject their Bible and their tradition, let us ask whether we in fact can do any differently. We may claim to believe the Bible or the teachings of the Church 'because they are true', and in some way believe that their truth somehow exempts us from a role in believing them, but can this be the case? Are we not all guilty of choosing our beliefs in all departments of life? In politics, sport, career, love, education, relaxation, as well as religion, are we not, in Jean-Paul Sartre's wonderful phrase, 'condemned to freedom'? Which is to say, 'condemned to choose'. That we have chosen a conservative, passive acceptance of the authority of Bible or Church no more means that we have not made a choice than if we choose to reject God, religion and faith of any kind altogether. What appear to be matters of faith become in these circumstances matters of politics, which is to say the way we deal with and respond to the prevailing opinions and powers of the world.

What about the Bible?

What right has anyone to set himself or herself over against the Bible when it comes to matters of belief?

Well of course I do not set myself over against the whole Bible; I am selective. And the basis of my selection is very much what defines the kind of Christian I am. I realize that for some the Bible is either right in its entirety or wrong, but I find that impossible to believe or even to understand. And in practice, even the most ardent fundamentalist still has favourite verses, passages and books, and so defines some part of the canon of Scripture as in a sense more important than other parts.

The Bible was written by human beings whose lives had been deeply affected by a certain set of experiences and a tradition which had thought and prayed a great deal about a particular version of God. The Hebrews, later the Jews, and finally the Christians, each had their own strands of thought and their own interpretations of events. Sometimes they were greatly weighed down by the injustices of the world, and wrote things that are hard to stomach (even if they are easy to understand). For example, the end of Psalm 137, which begins 'By the rivers of Babylon we sat down and wept when we remembered Zion' is (notoriously), 'happy is he . . . who seizes your infants and dashes them against the rocks'.

It is difficult to read or sing this verse without feeling very uncomfortable. But I would not want to eliminate it from the Bible because it reminds us of just how angry and vengeful human beings can be, and just how far we can be pushed by the treatment we have received in the world, and just how easily we can retaliate in kind. (The emphasis in this verse should be upon 'your'; the implication being that the Babylonians had already done the same to the children of the Jews.)

The Old Testament is full of slaughter and human destruction, and some of it is gloried over. (Psalm 58 is the great example, where the psalmist wishes upon the enemies of Israel the fate of the stillborn child that never sees the sun (v. 8), and the righteous man exults in victory by bathing his feet in the blood of the wicked (v. 10).)

What kind of authority do we allow such expressions of human anger? I think we allow them to be real, and therefore genuine outpourings of human emotion. But do we suppose them to be given God's approval because they appear in the Bible? Do we imagine (as many have done) that they justify imitating such actions or approving of such thoughts if we find ourselves in similar circumstances?

I am sure that the answer is no. But because they are there to be read, given special status by virtue of being present in the Bible, they require us to face such thoughts as they arise in us. The Bible does not allow us to run away from reality. 'All human flesh is here', including honest expressions of human destructiveness that we must learn to control if they are not to overwhelm us. And that alone is sufficient justification for retaining them in the Scriptures.

But that still leaves open the question of the authority of the Bible when we regard it as based upon the claim that its authors were inspired by God in a special way which gives their writings special authority over us.

What about Inspiration?

I do not find it possible to believe in the 'special' status of the writings we find in the Bible if that is supposed to place them above contradiction. That would mean that we have to accept them all or not at all. I emphatically deny the Bible such status. If 'special' is intended to mean that they are free from the errors that attend all human writing, then I deny them that status too. And one of my reasons is that to credit the Bible with such special status denies the role of the living, present God in the way that we read it. In other words, an infallible Bible diminishes the power of the present reality of God.

The Bible *is* special nonetheless. It is special because of the way it was written, and it is special because of the way it is read. Thousands and millions of people have read it and been ready to allow it to guide their lives. Generation after generation of human beings have read the Bible and lived by the Bible, reaffirming the wisdom found in its pages through their reading and obedience.

But they have not all read every page equally often, or treated every book with equal reverence, or given the same weight to every expression, or paid equal attention to every law and moral teaching. Neither should they have done. The fact that we have been moved to be selective in our reading of the Bible shows that God has not left us without guidance in the matter, as if the Bible were set irrevocably in stone for all time. So in effect the Bible is special because it is a convenient source of high-quality thoughts written by other human beings about the nature of life and the way to live it before God.

It is perfectly possible to imagine other collections of writings such as the Qu'ran, the Hindu scriptures, the writings of Guru Nanak and the teachings of the Buddha, as having an equal influence just because generation after generation have found guidance and comfort in them and so have recommended them to their children and shaped their societies by them. But such collections need not be exclusively religious. They may be of writings by other thinkers drawn from all over the world and from all sorts of backgrounds (Confucius, Marcus Aurelius, Plato, Aristotle, Maimonides, and so on, and modern writers like Barth, Eliot and Rilke in their different ways). Scientific and philosophical writings too can inspire and guide. The difference in the latter cases is that the collections are more diffuse and more recent, fewer people read each one, and so their influence is that much smaller. It is nevertheless perfectly possible to imagine that someone might write a book in the near future that will, one day, achieve the status of the Bible or the Qu'ran in the heart and minds of those who read it.

So in the sense that it is just a collection of writings written by fallible human beings, albeit writings of great antiquity and historical and religious importance, the Bible is no different from any other collection of such writings. Some parts of it are more valuable than others. (I challenge even the most convinced biblical fundamentalist to tell me or to believe that the lists of the generations of humankind, for example, or the blood-thirsty verses from the Psalms that I have cited, are equal in importance to the Gospels. Yet as soon as we make even so slight a distinction, everything concerning the relative importance of what is inside and outside the Scriptures is suddenly open to further revision – just as it should be.)

Does this view of inspiration undermine the special status of Jesus as well?

What about the Word become Flesh?

If the Bible, from which we learn of Jesus, is just one book among many, and its writings just one collection of imperfect writings, among many, that seems to imply that Jesus cannot be the special person we believe him to have been when we call him Son of God and Incarnate Word. We seem forced to say that Jesus is just another human being who lived a very good life and set us an example by his life and teaching, an example many have rightly felt that they wanted to follow. Jesus, on such a reading, becomes an example of how to live our lives, but no more.

I do not accept this conclusion for a moment, although it is very popular today. One of my reasons for rejecting it is that my belief in Jesus is not based upon the Bible directly. The Bible is a source which we come to and come back to in order to enrich our understanding of who Jesus is, but belief in Jesus really arises from a deep personal conviction based upon the feeling that in this one human being God came and lived as a human being.

It is wrong to approach this question as an intellectual or academic exercise. That is where many religious writers, theologians and scientists go wrong. Belief is not in the end based upon intellect; it is based upon the deep feelings that define who we are.

I have reached the stage in my own belief where knowing who I am and knowing who Jesus is are not really separable any longer. Those who suggest to me – friends and enemies – that I should abandon belief in the Incarnation because of recent New Testament scholarship, new insights in literary criticism, scientific objections to the possibilities of the virgin birth, the miracles and the resurrection, or because there are so many religions in the world that are excluded once I insist that Jesus is the one place in all history where God became man, make little or no impact upon me at all. Why not? Because belief in Jesus as the Son of God has nothing to do with this kind of intellectual analysis, and this kind of intellectual analysis is probably incapable of bringing us anywhere near to a full appreciation of the person of Jesus.

Jesus is the Incarnate Word, the Son of God, the one place in all history where we can look and find God and humanity fully together in one location and one life. I know this to be true because I am less certain of everything else that I might call true. I am more sure of this than I am sure of who I am, where I am, or what I am doing at this very moment. All these things may be illusions, but not this. The Jesus who is the Incarnate Word defines the truth, and sets down a measure against which all other claims to truth are to be understood and by which they all fall, including the truth about myself.

In other words, I have chosen to be a person for whom the question of the identity of Jesus of Nazareth, the Christ, the Son of the living God, is the first axiom, the first assumption, the starting-point of all else. Were I to cease to believe this, I would cease to be the person others know, the person I know, and the person I wish to be. And I am completely unapologetic about this stance because I am convinced that we each in fact take up such a stance over something, and because I am thankful that I have found my way to a stance with which I am completely comfortable and which I am entirely happy to have shape me to the roots of my being.

I lay claim to this as an absolute right because I have, by good fortune or the grace of God, found my way into a position in life where I am absolutely convinced that nothing in all creation can separate us from the love of God made known in Christ Jesus. I am, in that glorious phrase of the Authorized Version (and it does not matter very much to me whether or not it is a correct translation of the Greek), *persuaded* (Romans 8.38).

What worries me, however, is that there are many who have not found their way to this kind of deep and self-defining conviction. They have not realized that they have (by default) taken up a style of life that, if they knew there were alternatives, they would not in fact choose, and are as a result buffeted from pillar to post by 'the heartache and the thousand natural shocks that flesh is heir to' (*Hamlet*). What worries me, in other words, is the question of how we can introduce those who yearn for, and have not yet attained this vision, to the light that enlightens everyone who comes into the world. This light is the gift of the grace of God.

What about Grace?

As is so often the case, before we can obtain a clear view of the nature of grace we must clear away many misconceptions which have collected round it, and clarify and establish some distinctions which are necessary if we are to appreciate it. Some common misunderstandings are to see grace as a thing or substance, or as favour.

Most of the problems associated with grace arise from thinking of it as a substance which is transferred from God to his creatures. According to Aquinas, for example, sacraments cause grace, and for the Anglican Book of Common Prayer, following Augustine, the sacraments are an outward and visible sign of an inward, invisible grace. These notions, although they need to be hedged about with qualifications if they are to be understood with all the subtlety they deserve, generate a notion of grace as an essentially mechanical consequence of some kind of human action as a result of which grace is implanted or realized within another human soul.

A second misunderstanding of grace associates it with special blessing, a favour or reward from God for those things which we have done, a gift which transforms us according to the will of God which seeks to make in us some extra special person. Closely associated with grace as favour is the promise of future reward in which grace becomes an assurance of ultimate blessedness, a kind of delayed reward for services rendered, that serves little purpose other than to make us feel good about ourselves in spite of whatever present state we find ourselves in.

As in all things the place where we must first look for clues to the true nature of grace is the person of Jesus. Here, if at all, we must expect to find the life of one who lived by the grace of God. Here, then, immediately, we see the folly of the notion that grace involves a blessed earthly state made up of rewards, for here we find a man of sorrows, despised and rejected of men, and delivered up to death.

But equally immediately we see the key to the whole matter in the state of communion between humankind and God that is manifested in complete obedience and union of mind and purpose. Grace manifested itself in Jesus through his life and work. Grace, it seems, is not something tangible to be had, but something insubstantial to be seen and felt. As Wittgenstein once put it, it is something that can be shown but not said.

And this clue illuminates the matter, showing the connection with the great English Quaker George Fox's 'inner light', with Newman's 'illative sense', and with the sense of the presence of God that inspired and directed the prophets and saints in every age. Grace thought of in this way may be understood as real presence, vision and true blessing.

To speak of 'real presence' is to run the risk of further

confusions with Christian belief about the presence of Christ in the Eucharist, but in the present context the sense is, I imagine, clear. To live in a state of grace is to live in the real presence of God and to have his presence manifested through our lives, to ourselves and to others. The real presence of God in Jesus was thus the ultimate instance of divine grace made fully present on earth, for in Jesus that presence was embodied, incarnate.

For us the locus of such presence is seldom if ever the individual, however. Our post-Enlightenment obsession with the individual has led to an unacceptable diminution of the sense of what it is for God to be present, and we have tended to regard our sense of the presence of God in private terms, an ego trip for the spiritually fit and agile. That is a travesty of true grace. For, as in all things spiritual, the presence of God does not reside in one but in many, and our sense of that presence is mediated through the community composed by God's Holy Spirit as Church. The real presence of God in the world – in his creatures and in its processes – engenders a state of grace through which we can commune with him and be enlivened by him.

Only when we turn to consider the ways in which that presence is invisible to others of our species do we glimpse the proper sense in which for God to be 'there' he must also, and in a sense first, be 'here'. We see what we know. Buy a new Volvo and suddenly everyone is driving one. Without the real presence of God within us we will be incapable of discerning his presence in others and in the world. But without that presence in others and in the world our sense of God's presence in ourselves will be profoundly and perhaps fatally diminished.

The presence of God in each of us makes it possible for us to perceive that same presence in others – even and perhaps especially in those who do not perceive it in themselves. Grace is thus vision as well as presence.

Jesus' disciples were given to understand – to see – what to others was obscure. For the others it was a case of, 'though seeing, they may not see; though hearing they may not understand' (Luke 8.10; see Isaiah 6.9). Without grace there is no vision of God, no understanding of the world. And without that vision and understanding there is only and necessarily despair. For to hold out hope in the absence of God is to hold out for an illusion. Grace, and the absence of grace, are manifested in presence, or absence, of hope. To live in a state of grace is to be given sight and hearing.

But we must not allow ourselves to be carried away with a possessive, grabbing sense of achievement, as if to live in such a state were no more than a quick fix, a spiritually induced 'trip' to lift us out of our despondency.

Jesus' example comes to our aid again, perhaps especially, here. For in Jesus there was both the sight and the hearing: he saw the truth and he heard what the world perceived as truth as lies. His tears when he wept over Jerusalem were not the tears of one who merely agonized over the cruelty and inhumanity of the world, but the tears of one whose eyes saw also the emptiness of the world, the absence of grace manifested in failure to be aware of the presence of grace.

This vision sears the heart and tears at the soul. This vision shows us the lostness of the world, our own state of utter helplessness; and it gives and takes at one and the same time a sense of the awesome extent of human despair. The same grace which reveals that hopelessness also eliminates it. The same hands which place the yoke upon us also lighten it. With the vision comes true blessing.

We are now equipped to see the ambiguity of the gift of grace, the wish to receive grace, bestowed upon one another in blessing. 'The cup of blessing, which we bless, is it not a sharing of the blood of Christ; the bread which we break; is it not a sharing of the body of Christ?' This blessing of bread and cup is a blessing that leads to crucifixion and death. The blessing, this wish for the actualization of the state of grace which confers vision and realizes presence, is both a blessing and, in the world's sense at least, a curse. This is no easy wish, no slight offering, no mealy-mouthed spiritual lift. This blessing is a burden, a taking up of the cross, an exhortation to discipleship in which we will see the world as others do not see the world, and hear the world as others cannot hear the world. But what gives rise to this change in the way we see, this transformation of the way we hear? What brings about this conversion?

What about Conversion?

The fundamental problem in discussing the meaning of Christianity is that while we are working with other sets of rules – which may be intellectual or rational, literary, scientific, philosophical, emotional, psychological, sociological or whatever else – we are trying to judge the things of God (and therefore the things of Jesus) in terms of things that are less than God and inappropriate as ways to measure the truth that comes from God. 'Through God alone can God be known' (Emil Brunner, *The Mediator*).

The intellectual arguments against the Incarnation are legion. So are the literary, philosophical, scientific and religious arguments (the latter understood in terms of religious studies, which seeks to treat religions as comparable, and even sometimes equivalent, social phenomena).

So if we are facing the kinds of doubts with which all these arguments surround belief in Jesus as the Son of God, how on earth are we to find a way to suspend those doubts sufficiently to gain a glimpse of the glory that can resonate so powerfully in our hearts that we reach the point where we can feel the glory of God as its own reward, and the being of Jesus as the first principle that allows us to change our understanding of all other truth? In other words, how are we to be converted?

It is important that we do not begin by thinking that we need to be converted in order to be 'saved', in order to inherit everlasting life, or in order to comfort ourselves after some tragedy that leaves the maps we had made for ourselves about our future in tatters. Such things place the emphasis in the wrong place.

Conversion begins when we are ready to find our completeness outside ourselves. Fortunately, most of us know what it is like to love someone else, and so we know what it is like to care about someone else more than we care about ourselves. This is the model for belief. Although by stressing the sense in which 'I' make up 'my' mind about the kind of person 'I' want to be, I may have given the impression that this is very egocentric, a matter of having what I want, in fact by choosing to believe in something that matters more than my self, I turn this on its head.

So we cannot, in short, start on the road to conversion by being obsessively interesting in ourselves and in what we want for ourselves. We need to see the other whom we care about more than we care about ourselves as the first hint of what it is like to be converted, of what it is like to find a way to set aside our pride, our intellectual questions, our philosophical objections, our literary quibbles, our scientific theories. We need to learn to abandon everything that stands in the way of discovering a centre that is outside ourselves (even if, as I have said, the decision to do so starts from within).

What mostly stands in the way is, I think, our desire to remain in control. Those who want to share in the vision of God's glory through faith in Jesus also somehow want it to be their glory, something which they remain in control of, and therefore something that leaves them the same as they were (but happier, more fulfilled). Jesus realized that this cannot be the way. He put it in stark terms: we must abandon home and wife and family (Luke 14.26). We must give up everything we love for ourselves, discover the love that is based in others, and then find what we have given up restored to us. 'Whoever loses his life for my sake will find it' (Matthew 10.39 etc.) points us towards this (among other things).

Another way to look at this is to see conversion as a way of distinguishing two quite different kinds of love (one of which is not really love at all). To love another – wife, husband, child, friend – for oneself is to try to make them what we need them to be (or, which is worse, to try to keep them as they were when we first loved them). Such love stifles and kills not only the one whom we love, but ourselves, for we keep them the same in order to keep ourselves the same.

Love based upon and centred in the other allows the other to change and grows and rejoices in the other's change and growth. Such love finds itself enriched and strengthened by that change and growth because deeper and more fulfilling possibilities arise with the other as the other grows more mature. And the changes in the other bring about changes in ourselves. So conversion really begins when we accept that we can no longer live for ourselves or in ourselves and that we need to allow others to be what they are. Once we allow others to be what they are, they become able to help us to change. We find ourselves in the presence of those who can change us.

But a natural question to ask is, if this conversion is possible, and if I deeply desire it, why has it not happened? Why does God deny me the vision of his glory?

What about Me?

If I have taken everything that was said in the previous section to heart and yet still find that nothing happens, what am I to say? What can I do to bring myself into a new relationship with God in faith if it just does not happen? Perhaps we need to ask what is holding us back, and probably the only way to find that out is for each of us to seek out someone we really trust who does share in the vision of God's glory, and who will be willing to sit down with us (perhaps for a very long time) and talk through our problems.

The kind of person I have in mind is not overly concerned to convert anyone in the old-fashioned sense, and is not therefore an evangelical in the narrow sense of the word. He or she will not see conversion as a step in the direction of the salvation of a soul. He or she will not be anxious to achieve a 'quick fix'. On the contrary, such a person will not believe that our ability to perceive God's glory in this way matters other than in the sense in which it will make us a new creature (which therefore means that it matters a great deal). But becoming a new creature is not a qualification for salvation; it is one of the fruits of the salvation that has already been made possible by Jesus.

Jesus does not say, 'Come to me and then all your problems will evaporate.' Jesus says, 'God loves you; I love you; you are already saved; learn to live again in the power of that love.' That is what 'whoever believes in him shall have eternal life' (John 3.16) means. There is all the difference in the world between the two.

And it is also possible to try too hard. I have had friends who constantly ask about conversion, about why they cannot believe, about why despite their best efforts the faith that I have just will not come. They blame themselves; I blame myself. They think they've failed to do something; I think I've failed to say something.

It may just be that they are not ready, that they are struggling in the wrong way, that their motivation is wrong, or that I am the wrong person to help them. And yet it may also be that this torment (for such it can certainly be) is the darkness before the dawn. And it may be that they are looking for a sudden change in their entire outlook – a Damascus Road experience – when only something much more gradual is available. But relieved of the pressure of the notion that we need to believe in order to be saved, the whole process takes on a very different aspect.

Another way to see this is to put oneself in the position of the man or woman who seems to want to believe but cannot. 'Why, if there is a God, and I have prayed that he will grant me faith, do I not believe?' Some conclude from their inability to find faith that there cannot be such a God.

The tragedy of all this becomes clear when we see how this desperate search for faith has been generated and sustained by a wrongly understood Christianity. Where faith is regarded (as it so often is) as a necessary condition for salvation, almost as something we give God in return for salvation, it becomes something we want for quite the wrong kinds of reasons. It becomes a means we employ to hold on to ourselves as we are. Where faith is merely regarded as a way to experience deeper levels of spiritual wholeness, it becomes a way to satisfy selfish cravings that are anything but truly holy.

In other words, by teaching that faith is the way to salvation and that only through faith can we attain spiritual wholeness, we always run the risk of turning faith inside out. Instead of being a path to surrender of the self, it becomes a path by which we make our sense of self and our own importance stronger. We want faith the way we want a bigger car, a better hi-fi, or a larger house: because through it we become more comfortable (or so we assume). But what if faith and its fruits are not commodities to be bought and sold, and their effects on us quite other than we might wish for or imagine? What if faith has the opposite effect? What if through coming to faith, far from feeling more comfortable, we feel less? What if faith makes us sensitive and vulnerable to those aspects of the world we would rather keep buried, so that in faith we acquire not the skin of a rhinoceros, impervious to all that the world can do to us, but the wings of a butterfly that the slightest touch can damage or destroy?

And, of course, the question we then ask is why anyone in his or her right mind would be interested in acquiring such a faith. To which my reply would be, 'Yes, why would they?' Look at those whom God has called to his service, first awakening in them a sense of their own calling, their own contribution to God's work, then setting them upon a hard road. Consider the complaints and the laments, the excuses and the backslidings of the Hebrew prophets, who twisted and turned to try to escape from God's call. Consider those whom Jesus called to be disciples, and what their eventual fate proved in most cases to be. Then complain about why you cannot find faith despite all your beseeching and praying, and ask whether you are asking for what you want or what those whom God has called to his service have generally received. There is very little here that gels with the smug self-satisfaction of some of those most concerned to ask us whether we are 'saved'.

And the highest and most perfect of callings goes together with the highest and most perfect of faiths in Jesus of Nazareth whom we call the Christ. Yet even he prayed in Gethsemane that the cup which faith had poured out for him should pass from him if God so willed. But God did not so will.

What about Jesus?

Part of the problem we have with our beliefs is that Jesus seems to have called individual disciples directly, and they seem to have responded without hesitation - as in the story of the calling of Peter and Andrew. I am somewhat sceptical. This idea of an instant and unprepared conversion seems to have been told in a startling way, but how much actual historical detail has been omitted? We do not know, for example, whether the disciples had already heard Jesus preach, asked him questions, searched their hearts, and whether they needed just the added stimulus of the call to tip the balance.

Yet we equally have instances of what we call 'love at first sight' to indicate that it is possible, for we-know-not-what reasons, for two people to see one another and just 'know' that their lives have changed. In such circumstances, who are we to deny the possibility that the disciples were just 'ready', somehow in the right frames of mind to look upon Jesus and see him as the answer to the question of what they were to do with their lives. That is a perfectly credible scenario. There they were, mending their nets, when all of a sudden, there was someone standing by them in whom they instantly saw the answer to their prayers. 'Now I know what my life is all about!'

And it may also be that not all are called to be disciples in this way. It is easy to assume that God requires everyone to be a

Christian, and many who think that unless you are a Christian you are not saved certainly give their attention to trying to bring others on board the ark of salvation. But it need not be so.

For some of us the beliefs and the visions are not part of what will make up our lives, for a vision such as God's glory entails may send us off in directions in which we would be reluctant to travel. Those who are blessed with faith and visions of God's glory – if they are blessings, for as we have seen, they involve a heavy price in terms of what God may require of us in return for them – may simply be the leaven in the lump, those called upon to speak in God's name while others engage in the myriad other things that must be done if the world is to proceed upon its course.

That suggests that we are granted faith and vision for a purpose which is not at all what many Christians think it to be. The burden which is light is nonetheless a burden (Matthew 11.6), 'because the Lord disciplines those he loves, and he punishes everyone he accepts as a son' (Hebrews 12.6).

What about Fundamentalism?

For many Christians, a strong faith in Jesus is a guarantee of their own individual salvation. For them, Christianity has become no more than an extension of the western individual dream that sees success in terms of the success of individuals. 'Are you saved, brother?' becomes a distorted way of saying 'Are you saved *like me*, brother?' And what is going on here is often a rather unpleasant form of racism: an attempt to divide humanity up into two groups, except that rather than black and white, gentile or Jew (each of which divisions has caused more than enough human suffering), the division is now into those who are saved and those who are not.

The concerns of Christians who approach their faith this

way are largely with reassurance. Every chip that is knocked from the rock of Christian truth by science, philosophy, literary criticism, social theory and psychology becomes a personal assault. They rush to bookshops to purchase books to tell them that everything is really all right, and to churches to meet people and hear messages from preachers who tell them that all the evidence to the contrary notwithstanding, God remains in his heaven and all is right at least with them, if not with the world.

In these circumstances, the question, 'Are you a Christian?' serves the same purpose as the questions, 'Are you a Freemason?' or, 'Are you a Jew?' It is designed to determine whether you are inside or outside some group which is supposed to divide one kind of human being from another. To hesitate to give a reply (usually because just this doubt is present in one's mind) is to be condemned immediately: anyone who is not sure whether he or she is a Christian is not a Christian.

The trouble is that it just is not clear what being a Christian means in this context. Very often it involves a kind of biblical fundamentalism in which the Bible is taken to hold the answers to all important questions, and where belief that the Bible contains the answers to all important questions is itself a necessary part of the faith that saves.

There is more wrong with this view than can be seen from recognizing that the Bible, as the work of fallible human beings, may be deeply flawed in many respects. Or that the Bible cannot be exempt from the kind of critical analysis that we extend to other written works. Such convictions about the Bible are mistaken. What is perhaps even more worrying however is the way, by believing in the infallibility of the Bible, we give up some of the responsibilities that go with being human. Responsibilities for deciding what is right and wrong, true and false, worthy and unworthy of honour and praise, allegiance and denial, for example.

'Are you a Christian?' amounts on this kind of reading to something like, 'Are you rich?' or, 'Do you have a television?' It sets up a notion of Christianity in which we see faith as a possession, certainty and comfort as a right. And in return for such certainty and assurance we are prepared to surrender our freedom, which is to say to surrender that about us which most makes us human.

This is a very serious issue. Many religious groups are built around a widespread human need to give up aspects of our freedom. We want to give it up because we are frightened by it, by the responsibilities it involves, and by the errors into which we can fall when we exercise it. The Russian writer Fyodor Dostoevsky, in one of the most perceptive passages on this subject in all literature, put into the mouth of his Grand Inquisitor in *The Brothers Karamazov* the view that human beings are all-too-ready to surrender their freedom to the Church in exchange for peace of mind. Biblical fundamentalism (whether in the mainstream churches or sects like the Jehovah's Witnesses with their own idiosyncratic interpretations of the texts) exchanges certainty for freedom. It trades on our need to be secure and our willingness to be comfortable even at the expense of being wrong.

But perhaps the biggest objection of all to biblical fundamentalism is that it denies something about God. It denies that God is genuinely present in the hearts and minds of all his creatures, ready to guide them even in pastures where the Bible has nothing to say. So fundamentalism actually involves denying ourselves and God at the same time by seeking to locate certainty somewhere other than in God and our own relationship with him. Biblical fundamentalism is a form of unbelief. And it is doubly an act of unbelief when it makes belief in the inerrancy of the Bible itself an article of faith necessary for salvation.

What about Worship?

At the other end of the scale from those who place all their faith in the words of the Bible there are those who replace the certainty and security of biblical fundamentalism with the certainty and security of regular worship. Sometimes that worship is eucharistic, sometimes not. It may be from a high or a low church position, Protestant or Roman Catholic.

Worship is, however, a very peculiar thing. If I were convinced that it always involved a process in which human beings in community came to share in a real, living experience of the vision of God's glory in and through Jesus Christ, I would have no hesitation in agreeing that worship is the very essence of Christian believing, the power source from which all Christian living draws its strength. Unfortunately, from my own experience at least, there is very little in what passes for Christian worship that involves anything remotely like encounter with the living reality of God, a vision of his glory in Christ, or anything that seems to make much of a contribution to human growth as God's children.

Much worship is dull. Some of it is damaging. Occasionally it is scarcely recognizable as a Christian activity at all. So why do we continue to engage in it?

I think that the vast majority of Christians continue to worship *despite* what worship is like rather than *because* of what it is like. And I believe that they do so for one or both of two reasons: either because they believe that God requires them to worship him; or because they need the reassurance that comes from doing something that many others do.

Worship, if understood the first way, is a modern equivalent of the animal sacrifice we find in the Old Testament: it is painful, unpleasant, dull, costly, sometimes frightening and even on occasion soul-destroying, but it is what God wants. There may even be those who think that because it is so unpleasant or unsatisfactory by all other standards, its value is increased. (I cannot suppress amazement at the kind of God those concerned must believe in to make such an argument believable.)

Of course there is worship that is quite different, that does involve a free coming-together of fellow Christians to share in the glory of God, and which also satisfies the various degrees to which we need one another's faith to reassure ourselves about our own. Such worship no doubt fills God's children with his love and renews and refreshes them. Such worship is not required; it is given. We come before God even though God does not require us to do so, and God fills our hearts and minds with his care and love. Nothing could be more natural; nothing could have less in common with the worship of those who believe that God will be angry with them if they fail to go to church, or that their salvation hangs upon attending a large number of soul-crushing services which count as the sacrifice of a broken spirit which the Lord will not despise.

The latter kind of worship is a travesty of genuine worship. And genuine worship need not take the form of congregational singing, praying and adoring at all. Where the hearts and minds of men and women assume a form in which they are defined by the nature and being of God in Jesus Christ, there worship is genuine, full and profound. But attend most churches (of whatever denomination) and that is not what we will find, and we will not emerge from the building refreshed in body and mind, charged with the glory of God, or even much closer to our neighbour. At best we will go home with the feeling that we have 'done our duty' and that God will be satisfied for another week. (If someone has a really bad case of religious paranoia they may feel obliged to repeat this self-destructive process more often, of course.)

In the sense in which worship involves the subservient singing of hymns and uttering of praise and adoration to God, I see no reason for it at all. In fact I see every reason to discourage it at every opportunity, for such worship denies that vision of the glory of God which is uniquely Christian: a vision of God not as Lord and Master, but as brother and friend. But that is not to say that we should discourage true worship – once we have discovered what it is.

The only true worship, as the Christian faith has always insisted in its best traditions, is the worship of Jesus the man. This worship consists purely and simply of obedience to the divine will. The worship of Jesus and the life of Jesus are not separable. Jesus does not worship God when he enters the synagogue on the sabbath day in some way that is fundamentally different from the way he worships God while wandering through the towns and villages of Galilee. And what is true of Jesus must also be true of us.

The worship of a Christian consists purely and simply in the life that Christian leads. Part of that worship, but only a part, may consist of gathering together to sing hymns, participate in the Eucharist, read the Bible and say corporate prayers. But it need not do so, and any suggestion that we fall short of God's expectations if we fail to do so must be countered at every turn. Justification for attending or not attending organized, institutional worship of this kind stands or falls over the question of God's presence in our lives in a way which makes obedience, and therefore the living of the life God wants us to live, possible.

What about God the Father?

I do not want my children to worship me. Why, then, do we suppose that God requires the worship of his children, if worship is understood in the terms described just now? Is it that we are projecting upon God the kind of desire for heartfelt gratitude and a sense of indebtedness that we like to engender in other human beings towards ourselves?

Of course there are parents whose principal objectives in raising their children are chosen from among the following: to instil a sense of gratitude; to live the lives they did not manage to live themselves through their children; to control their children; to make their children fear them; to make their children love them; to make their children idolize them. In each case, if the parents understand God to be to them as they are to their children (a very natural piece of psychological projection which one scarcely needs to read Sigmund Freud to understand), they will only deem themselves adequate children acceptable to God if they behave as they would have their own children behave. They want their children to do exactly as they are told, so they imagine that God is pleased when we do exactly what we are told (by the Bible or the Church). The Bible and the Church both tell us that God requires worship and sacrifice (even, in some interpretations, that God requires the sacrifice of the life of his own dear Son in the most ghastly and painful of circumstances).

For Christians of this persuasion (and for members of other religions), congregating together to tell God how wonderful he is, however dull such services of worship may be, is something we do because God requires it of us. But let us stop and think for a moment. What kind of God is it that we think we are worshipping in this way? If even human parents (some human parents) can rejoice in the growth into freedom and independence of their children, rather than requiring eternal devotion to their parents in return for 'all that the parents have done for them', on what possible basis do we imagine that the Creator of heaven and earth will not do the same?

How can we possibly imagine that God has the slightest interest in the singing of hymns, the saying of prayers, the preaching of sermons and even the reading of the Bible and the murmuring of the mass, in circumstances from which to all intents and purposes any semblance of a vision of his glory is absent from the minds of the participants? The kind of worship that is offered to God as sacrifice and duty arises from a thoroughly unworthy conception of who God is, and manifests by its mechanical and resentful mediocrity a complete absence of any true vision of God's glory.

This must not be misunderstood. It simply *must not* be misunderstood. There is no suggestion here that this kind of pointless worship is to be identified with poor singing, cold churches, mumbling parsons, hesitant prayers, and small congregations. It is perfectly possible that 'where two or three come together in my name' and there isn't a decent singer, reader, preacher or prayer among them, that there is a vision of

God's glory the like of which fails to shine in the finest and most richly endowed cathedral in the land.

What is at stake here has nothing to do with outward show, expressions of devotional fervour, manifestations of the spirit through 'speaking in tongues', vast congregations of young people clapping their hands and praising the Lord, or even with that most obvious feature of the newly born, 'bright singing'. It may have to do with all these things, and the vision of God's glory may well manifest itself in these ways, but we should not be overly willing to assume that where there is ecclesiastical smoke there must necessarily be spiritual fire.

Yet we train ourselves to believe the opposite. 'The sacrifice of God is a broken spirit; a broken and contrite heart he will not despise' (Psalm 51.17) we hear the Prayer Book tell us. Magnificent poetry, but what does it mean, and should we believe it? 'For Christ, our Passover lamb, has been sacrificed. Therefore let us keep the Festival' (1 Corinthians 5.7). But what kind of a God desires such sacrifice? And was the conviction of the Hebrews in the wilderness and the Jews of the Temple that God required sacrifice no more than an early aberration which has regrettably lingered on into our own attitude to worship? An attitude, that is, that thinks that the more painful and costly something is, the more God enjoys it? What kind of a God is that?

What about the Crucifixion?

The most obvious, and indeed the central, example of the relationship of God to sacrifice is in the crucifixion of Jesus. For almost all of human history, Jesus' death has been seen in terms of a sacrifice which appeases God, takes away our guilt, and so pays the price for our sins. There have been technicalities: sacrifices which appease God; sacrifices which substitute something else for the one against whom God is angry; sacrifices which pay the price demanded by God's sense of justice (that we are so sinful that we deserve to die, so somebody has to die even if not us).

The theme that runs through all this (a thoroughly understandable theme in view of the central place of sacrifice in Jewish religious practice before and during the first century, that is, the time during which the formative attempts were made to understand the death of Jesus in some sort of positive terms) is that God requires some kind of balancing price to be paid for the things that we do wrong.

I think that this is a dangerous and profoundly misleading idea. Here again I do not wish to be misunderstood, but this time my concern is not that I will be heard to say something I do not believe; it is that I will not be heard to say what I do believe. Which is this.

God has no interest whatever in sacrifice. Jesus' death is wrongly understood as a sacrifice (however it is interpreted). There is nothing that we can offer or are required to offer God in return for forgiveness for our sins.

God wants for us his children exactly what we want for our children: full and abundant life; freedom, independence, wholeness, joy. And all these things come not from sycophantic attention to supplying God's praise and adoration, but from learning to live our lives in light provided by the abundance of God's glory.

Why, then, did Jesus die? Because, in the words of John's Gospel, 'he came to that which was his own, but his own did not receive him' (John 1.11). And why did they not receive him? Because he threatened to overturn the social, political and religious structures of his day by insisting that 'whoever wants to become great among you must be slave of all' (Mark 10.44).

In this one saying, Jesus sealed his own death-warrant, for implicit in this saying is a complete change in not just the notion of earthly power (secular and religious) but in the notion of divine power and therefore actually of God. The one who clung not to equality with God but humbled himself

(Philippians 2.8) did the very thing that he told those who heard him they had to do. He who was greatest - God - became servant of all. And so the vision of God which fuelled and supported social and political structures that mean that the higher up you go the less of a servant and the more of a master you become, structures which believed themselves to be building earthly power on the basis of their vision of heavenly power, was turned upside down.

Worship, in other words, understood as giving God what he demands as his due, serves to underwrite a social, political and religious hierarchy in which those who are high up in the structure have a right to demand subservience, gratitude and honour from those below them *as their due*. God - in this scheme of things - ordains some to be kings and queens, who as such have divine rights. Kings and queens bestow favours on their nobles in return for loyalty, fealty and the honour due to them. Their nobles bestow honours on landowners, thence on labourers, and finally on the peasants and the beggars at the bottom of the pile who do all the dirty work and owe honour to everyone above them.

This view of society works until one of the beggars turns out to be the living Word of God. That really puts the cat among the pigeons. Especially when he seems to have powers which he could use to assume earthly ascendancy, taking his place at the top of the pile (but refuses to use them), and even more so when he stirs up the people with righteous indignation against the oppression of the political and religious powers of the day.

Jesus was crucified for being the Son of God, for the God whom he made present in his own life here on earth was no more an acceptable God in the first century than he is today. Jesus was not crucified in order to satiate the lust for compensatory blood in a tyrant who would otherwise have destroyed the earth. He was killed in a vain attempt by the ruling powers to hide the fact that such a tyrant does not exist, and that the social and political and religious structures which purport to be established in that God's name are unnecessary and unjustifiable.

There will be those who feel that I have been unfair to worship as it is experienced and practised by most Christians. It may be the case that most Christians have been fortunate to discover places of worship which satisfy all the positive criteria I have described and none of the negative ones. In that case my own experience of Christian worship has been very unrepresentative. But let us put this behind us. Let me try to say here what the positive criteria really amount to by dwelling on the subject of divine presence a little longer. How are we to understand the presence of God? What is it like to be in the presence of God? Where and when and how does a sense of that presence arise?

What about Presence?

Let me earth this discussion in a personal experience.

For the past ten years I have visited a community of contemplative Anglican nuns regularly to celebrate the Eucharist. I have officiated at most of the higher festivals of the year, been introduced to some of what are for me the more arcane rites of the liturgical calendar, and been privileged to be invited to conduct numerous quiet days for them and to give various talks.

None of this would be remarkable were it not for the fact that I am not of their liturgical persuasion at all. That much must be obvious from what has gone before. I understand their contemplative life, but I could not share in it. I understand and respect their liturgical practices (my approach to such matters is pragmatic – I do as I am told; I am, after all, among them as one who serves), but I cannot say that I derive much inspiration from them. They know this as well as I do. I make no attempt to pretend that I understand what they ask me to do, although it would be putting it far too strongly to say that I do not approve. However, during a short address I once gave there, the following thought occurred to me.

When we visit places we have not been to for some time, we rediscover parts of ourselves which we left behind there. These contemplative nuns now hold a part of me in their community which I value, which I did not know to be part of me before I encountered them, and which they have given me reason enough to believe that they value as well. When I am away from them it is hard to recapture what it is that resides there, but I think that it has something to do with mutual acceptance through and despite difference. By being what they are and by being what I am, we find ourselves mutually enriched. I am able to be someone there that I cannot be elsewhere; they, through the echoes of my self they hold there, and through the enrichment of those echoes that comes from what they are, enable me to reach parts of myself that other experiences do not enable me to reach.

This begins to make sense of worship as ritual, as service, as ceremony. If we are fortunate enough to find somewhere that makes it possible for us to reach more deeply into ourselves, there we are most likely to find God waiting for us. Just as certain art, certain literature, certain music affords us a way of making contact with that depth in ourselves and in the world that is otherwise so elusive, so certain ceremonies can, if approached in the right way, put us in touch with the depths of ourselves in ways that are impossible otherwise.

It is this experience - by whatever resources it is enabled - that must have inspired the psalmist to write what is perhaps the greatest of all the psalms, Psalm 139 which I quote from the Authorized Version, which strikes me as incomparable:

> O Lord, thou has searched me, and know me.
> Thou knowest my downsitting and mine uprising, thou understandest my thought afar off.
> Thou compassest my path and my lying down, and art acquainted with all my ways.
> For there is not a word in my tongue, but, lo, O Lord, thou knowest it altogether.

Thou hast beset me behind and before, and laid thine hand upon me.
Such knowledge is too wonderful for me; it is high, I cannot attain unto it.
Whither shall I go from thy spirit? or whither shall I flee from thy presence?
If I ascend up into heaven, thou art there: if I make my bed in hell, behold, thou art there.
If I take the wings of the morning, and dwell in the uttermost parts of the sea;
Even there shall thy hand lead me, and thy right hand shall hold me.
If I say, Surely the darkness shall cover me; even the night shall be light about me.
Yea, the darkness hideth not from thee; but the night shineth as the day: the darkness and the light are both alike to thee. (Psalm 139.1–12)

True worship cannot be defined by the boundaries of churches or the rules of the canon lawyers. But when we are able, perhaps not to write – that would be to ask too much – but at least to read words such as these, and feel ourselves questioned to the very roots of our being, there worship takes place. For in the encounter with God that is made possible by such words we find ourselves placed in touch with the height and depth of all creation. And in that touch we are changed.

What about Transformation?

Most of us know people with whom we like to be, and places where we like to go, because when we are with them, and when we are there, we feel more alive. Friends bring about a change in us. We find that in their company we can feel things – parts of them, parts of ourselves – which we cannot reach when we are apart. Many people, places and things have this power to call up from the depths of our being those precious treasures which lie dormant as we go about our humdrum daily lives. If we are fortunate, we find daily lives which keep us in touch with them all the time.

This kind of change – that I am most fully what I am when I am with you – is what I understand by conversion. We each become most fully what we are when we are with God in the community of our fellow men and women. This experience is the occasion for true rejoicing, and therefore true worship: 'I rejoiced with those who said to me, "Let us go to the house of the Lord"' (Psalm 122.1). I was glad when the Lord came into my life and made me whole. I was glad when I met someone whom I loved or came to love. I was glad to be helped and enabled to be what I most fully am.

This kind of change, contrary to what we so often suppose about conversion, is far from permanent. Its very nature means that it comes and goes with the friends who come and go, the places we must visit and leave. God may always be with us, but he is not always with us in ways that make a difference of the kind I am talking about.

The occasion of true worship is the occasion of my reconversion – yearly, weekly, daily, hourly – from what I am that I would rather not be into that self I can occasionally just glimpse when I am able to reach my deepest depths. I imagine that for those for whom a daily Eucharist or the daily office or the discipline of the canonical hours is most dear, it is this experience of being lifted out of and up from oneself that is sought (even if it is not always found).

With certain people, performing certain actions, and in certain places, we are transformed. For some – myself included – institutional worship fails to have this effect. Those of us who are in this position are likely to seek those people, actions and places which put us most fully in touch with what we are in other ways. I refuse – and I mean refuse – to believe that we are therefore in some kind of inferior position, or that the fullness that we can and do find is any less true worship because it does not conform to the patterns of a church. In fact, I feel rather the opposite to be the case: it would be a sin against God to persist in engaging with a person, a practice or a place which, far from putting us in touch with our deepest selves, had been found to blot out each self and distance us from the transformation that can alone be found in true communion.

Our response to true transformation is to do what God would have us do; to obey what we learn of God's will for us as it makes itself known through our worship and manifests itself in our ministry. The realization of the fruits of true transformation in a transformed life is the only way that we can test whether we have indeed been changed. And in order to understand how best we can both change and be changed, it may first be necessary to consider what is involved in true Christian ministry.

What about Ministry?

We may classify ministry in two ways.

Priestly ministry sees itself doing for members of religions what they cannot do for themselves. The High Priest of the Hebrews entered into the Holy of Holies to make atonement for the people who could not enter in for themselves. Priesthood is associated in most religions with sacrifice, with placing something before God instead of the people themselves in an effort to placate, appease or please him. In its mildest form, priesthood involves praying on behalf of the people, and even instead of the people, offering to God what the people do not, because of their forgetfulness, their idleness, their indifference or their unbelief, offer him for themselves.

Rabbinic ministry involves teaching others to do things for themselves (although no doubt some rabbis assume more priest-like roles). Jesus was a true rabbi in that he gave those who heard him responsibility for their own lives and their own beliefs. Jesus was a true priest in that he did for us what we genuinely could not do for ourselves.

Although the term 'priest' has innocent uses that mean little more than 'fully ordained minister', it is frequently used of those who do indeed see their role in terms of doing for others what they cannot do for themselves, and it sometimes spills over into preventing others from doing what they could do for themselves if they were encouraged a little. The priest, in this sense, engenders a passive spirit among Christians because he perceives himself as standing between them and God, and his congregation as those upon whose behalf he says prayers. Yet the effect of this is to introduce two classes into Christian life, the ordained and the lay, those especially blessed and those who are not, and it is far from clear that this is a healthy division to introduce into the Christian Church.

The notion of someone who does for God's children what they could in fact do for themselves seems to me to be infantilizing, a way of preventing Christians from growing up, a way of keeping them quiescent and inactive. This is particularly obvious where members of congregations find their priests unwilling (or unable) to answer their questions about the faith, and themselves in receipt far too often of answers which simply say that such-and-such is what the Church teaches so we must believe it. It is no wonder that so many people have deserted the churches if this is the best that they can do.

A rabbinic style of ministry turns this process round. Rather than viewing himself as standing between the people and God, the rabbi thinks only of serving them, educating them, and making them more and more able to stand on their own. Doubtless there are rabbis who use their position in other ways and for less worthy ends, but the principle persists. They are teachers and servants; they are not mediators (those who see themselves as standing between the congregation and God).

A rabbi has constantly to prove worthy of the role by exercising ministry in a way that makes a difference to his people, whereas a priest tends to assume that by virtue of his ordination he is entitled to their respect.

I am deeply unhappy about priestly ministry where it takes a form in which it sees itself in terms of doing for Christians what they cannot do for themselves or as standing between human beings and God. I do not see how the result can be anything less than a kind of second-hand Christianity in which we effectively pay someone to be a Christian for us. Priestly ministry (understood as a type of ministry and not as a slur cast against those who happen to be called priests even though they are in effect rabbis) seem to suppose that we are still in need of a barrier between ourselves and God. And therefore it retains a sense that God is a terrible figure whom we cannot come near. For the priest the veil of the temple has been restored to its former seamless state and only he and his kind are allowed to enter into the presence of God.

So, to justify an argument against priestly ministry as that which sees itself in terms of doing for others what they cannot do for themselves by standing between human beings and God, we need to ask the biggest question of all.

What about God?

What kind of God do we believe in? It seems such an easy question to answer. We need merely recite one of the creeds. 'We believe in God the Father almighty, . . .'. But do we, and should we? Have we even given any thought to the question whether such a notion makes sense?

The notion that God, in order to be God, must be all-powerful, all-knowing and everywhere-present, owes more to what we need God to be than to what God needs to be, namely self-subsistent (the source of his own being) and possessed of certain powers which cannot be determined just by what we think 'God' needs to be.

There has always been a conflict between theoretical and revealed notions of God in religious thought. Theory might say that God needs to be all-powerful; experience might say that he seems not to be. Theory might say that God can do anything; experience might indicate that he is very particular about what he does. The God whom Christians believe to have been revealed in Jesus sits uncomfortably with the God of the philosophers. Yet somehow the two have come to be equated, and it has been assumed that to believe in one is to believe in the other. 'It all depends upon what you mean by "God"' may seem a rather lame reply to questions about one's beliefs, but it is absolutely necessary. The God who is all-powerful, all-knowing and everywhere-present, and the God whose Word is incarnated and crucified, need not be the same.

God has to be the source of his own existence because that is the only way to avoid the infinite regress of 'Who made God?' God must be uncaused and unoriginate in order to be God. But such a God need not be all-powerful, and limitations upon his power need not be restricted only to those that would involve logical impossibility or self-contradiction: there may perfectly reasonably be things which an everlasting God simply cannot do. This offends us, of course, and will no doubt continue to give offence and lead some to reach for their dictionaries of heresy, because *we need God to be otherwise*. But our needs are not good reasons for attributing things to God unless we have already in some covert way allowed God to be no more than what we make him (and that is an insidious form of atheism). It may be part of the politics of religion to say that God is all-powerful, but it is not part of the logic of religion, and certainly not of revealed religion. In other words, to deny or at least question God's omnipotence may be to risk charges of heresy and to face religious ostracism, but that is a matter of politics, not theology.

Knowledge is always closely associated with power. The whims of political and religious leaders dictate what the churches teach, not the religious truths arising out of the heart-felt cries of God's children, struggling to live their lives in sometimes intolerable circumstances. Things 'cannot be said', not because they are not or cannot be true, but because it is too dangerous to say them, because the powers of the world wish to preserve themselves by defining 'God' in a certain way, and so giving divine authority to their knowledge. Church and State collude in claiming knowledge of 'what God would have us do', because to acknowledge the possibility that the people might have a better idea of what God would have us do would perhaps unsettle and even overturn the social order. 'Violence is the last refuge of the incompetent', as Isaac Asimov once put it. In other words, when we have lost every rational argument and failed in every possible way to persuade others to adopt our point of view about such a central matter as the nature of God, we turn to violence. You may not be persuaded by my arguments, but you will be persuaded by rack and fire and the threat of hell.

So let us suppose that God has certain powers, which include the power to generate universes such as ours, but not necessarily to know everything that may transpire in them, to control everything that happens in them, or to be present everywhere within them. Then God is faced with a dilemma: is a universe created with only partial knowledge and the possibility of partial input from its Creator still worth creating? Is such a God likely to leave himself open to the charge that he is incompetent or doesn't care? A Creator who creates despite being unable to predict, control or dwell fully in such a universe takes a risk, not only with it and whatever creatures may emerge from it, but with himself. For the creatures that it produces may well call to their God only to find him silent and impotent. They may well scream in agony out of their suffering, as the children of the holocaust and other victims of human bestiality down the centuries have screamed to their mothers and fathers under torture and in the grip of disease and death only to find them powerless to help. Is such a world worth creating? In the last analysis, *is the chance of life better than no chance at all?*

To answer 'Yes' to such a question is to commit oneself to an ultimate act of faith born of love. Despite all the pain that may be associated with it, life is to be cherished and fought for, to be risked as an ultimate gamble, and if the universe is to be the vehicle for life, then if life is good, the end must justify the means. A species capable of contemplating futility is faced with exactly the same choice. Ultimately, when all is said and done, do we as human beings believe in life, in regeneration, in our children and in the future, or are we concerned with nothing more than wallowing in the past and what Stevie Smith called so bitterly and powerfully 'our own mental stink' (*Analysand*)?

The God of the Hebrews and of Jesus Christ – the biblical God – answered 'Yes' to the question about the chance of life being better than no chance at all, even if aspects of that life would lie beyond that God's direct control and permit barbarity of a kind and on a scale that would unhinge any right-thinking person. For Christians, the hope such a God offers us is represented in the person of his Son, as Word made flesh, who lives and dies our life in order to ratify and affirm its ultimate value. Without that we do not even have a God who cares, and a God who does not care is infinitely terrible, for he is one who creates and then absconds.

Of course, this too is to define the God in whom we believe in terms of some notion of the God in whom we are willing to believe, but religious beliefs embraced in freedom are always in just this sense self-constitutive. Those who need to believe in a God who is all-powerful, all-knowing and everywhere-present define themselves as a certain kind of person. Those who choose not to believe in God at all do likewise. Those for whom the only God worth believing in is the God revealed in Jesus Christ shape their fundamental being in so doing. Jesus may not be the God we all want, but he is the only God we need, and certainly a better God that we deserve.

Perhaps what has made the notion of divine omnipotence so attractive to every generation is that human beings, deeply conscious of their own impermanence and frailty, find it hard to conceive of a love so great that it would be prepared to create that which it would not be able to control (despite the fact that all parents know exactly the pain such love entails). So God (we say) must be everywhere, knowing everything and controlling everything, because we, like a paranoid dictator with armies of secret police, would feel insecure were we not 'in control' in such a way.

Equally, there must be many for whom the real motive for belief in God lies in their understanding of his power and their hope that God can somehow be persuaded to use that power on their behalf. Although there are many good reasons why we are drawn to go to church in time of war and crisis, there are also many bad ones. Some no doubt believe that their church-going will help keep God on their side, persuade him to fight for their armies, protect their loved ones, even deal particularly mighty blows against the enemy. I have to say that I do not believe any of this for one minute. That is not the God in whom I believe. The God in whom I believe is insulted by such cheap worship.

An idea of God which allows God to be God without insisting that he be vested with the kinds of attributes which human beings would want to have if they were God, offers the world a radical alternative to its usual ideas of power and glory. Such a God's love is more powerful than his power, and his concern to create life greater than his need to control it or his urge to destroy it.

To be a Christian is not – or at least should not be – to adopt a belief that we think will ensure our everlasting life; it is to make a fundamental statement about life, to be prepared to look the world in the face and to go on believing in that world – as God believes in the world – even and perhaps especially when it behaves at its worst. It is to be prepared to love even and perhaps especially those who will only respond to love with hate, to freedom with cruelty, and to life with death. In other words, to be a Christian is to place oneself in a position not so very different from God's position as revealed in Jesus, and to be committed to love even when it leads to one's own humiliation and crucifixion. It is even to love those who, recognizing that vulnerability, will take advantage of it to make the humiliation greater and the crucifixion more agonizing. Few of us come anywhere near to that ideal. Many of us want God to be powerful enough to do everything we would like to have done, including bringing terrible and swift retribution on our enemies, the scorners, scoffers and nose-pickers of the world. The God of love does not yearn to be that powerful, for he never stops hoping that the lost will be redeemed.

In the choice between giving the universe the chance of life at the price of suffering with it, and creating no universe at all, what else could a loving God do, and what other kind of God would we do better to believe in?

What about Suffering?

I have offered a bold alternative to traditional thinking about God by suggesting that God may not after all be all-powerful, if by 'all-powerful' we mean 'able to do anything and everything'. I have acknowledged that to remove this feature of God may remove a major reason why some believe in him. I have suggested that, although the idea has a long history and a noble tradition, there is in fact absolutely no reason to suppose that God is anything like this. All we need suppose is that God is powerful enough to have created the universe, loving enough to enter into it in Jesus in order to share our existence, and faithful enough to remain true to us even when it involves his own immense pain and death in the crucifixion.

Is this an adequate answer to those who have endured and continue to endure great pain, who suffer at the hands of nature or at the hands of other human beings, and who die sometimes in agony and despair? For me the question hangs on the question I asked a moment ago: is the chance of life better than no chance at all? Does the choice between our universe, with nature 'red in tooth and claw', and no universe, vindicate God? Is it even comprehensible that God would be able to make our universe but not be able to make an even better one in which there was much less pain and suffering?

These are serious questions, and they must not be answered

lightly, especially not by someone for whom experience of sorrow, pain, suffering and death has not been great. But I am constantly and repeatedly assailed by those who do suffer, or know someone who has suffered, or have friends and relatives who have died, often in great pain, and who demand of me an answer to the question, 'Why doesn't God do something about it?'

I have pondered the question long and hard, and I have come to the conclusion that *God does all he can*. By this I mean not only that God does all that is within his power (which may, as I have suggested, be limited), but also that God does all that he can do without breaking the fabric of the universe he has made or tearing apart the subtle structure of the lives of his creatures.

It is easy – too easy, in my view – to overlook the possible consequences for the human race of tiny changes in the circumstances that define our lives. There would be no good reason, for example, to suppose that God would intervene to alleviate *this* pain without supposing that he would intervene to alleviate *all* pain of that severity. But then lesser pains would become the next candidates for his intervention, and soon we would be asking that all pain be eradicated.

Yet pain makes the world go round. Life as we know it would be completely altered if there were no pain. Our lives from the cradle to the grave are dictated by the need to manage, avoid, minimize or relieve pain. As I argue in *God and the Mind Machine* (SPCK 1996), the evolution of conscious self-awareness, of an inside-looking-out attitude to the world, may be dependent upon the presence of pain to prick us into such awareness. The development of a sense of self may have depended upon the need to avoid as much pain as possible. So there is no obvious way in which this pain or that could be alleviated without the whole fabric of human life being changed; its development might even have been made impossible in the absence of pain.

The same can be said of suffering which is not directly the product of physical pain. Mental anguish, worry, anxiety and the means we employ to deal with them are centrally important in our development as human beings. To suggest that we might live without such suffering would be to suggest that we might be completely different kinds of creatures.

My argument that God does all he can does not therefore diminish the scale of human suffering; neither does it eliminate the hope that on some occasions God may do more than we know. Who can say what God has done? Who can say what God is doing? Who can say what God will do? All we can say is that there are very cogent reasons why God does not do all we might in our less reflective or more desperate moments wish for (such as eliminate all pain, or even all death), and that there is no good reason to doubt that what he can reasonably and consistently do, he does.

What about Death?

Mention of death raises further questions for those who are convinced by the theory of evolution (even if only in its broad outline).

Evolutionary theory places death, not life, at the centre of the stage. Without death and the struggle for survival, there would be no selection of the fittest for survival, and hence no selection of the genes of those that survive so that they (and not less strong, less subtle, less flexible, less intelligent, or less whatever-it-might-be) creatures reproduce. Evolution envisages a cut-throat world in which thc weakest go to the wall and ruthlessness rules in all but the most extraordinary circumstances. So when we read 'the last enemy to be destroyed is death' (1 Corinthians 15.26), we read something that sits uncomfortably with modern evolutionary theory in which death is not an enemy, but the basis of all progress and development.

St Paul, of course, sees things in terms of human death and the potential end of all that we strive for. He is confronted by the almost obscene waste that death entails, when all that each human being has achieved and learned is reduced to nothing: 'Dust you are and to dust you will return' (Genesis 3.19) is a wonderful, moving, depressing summary of all that life and death entail. From Genesis to Revelation it is the same story: we are born and we live and we die.

What are we to say about death? Like physical pain and mental anguish, death colours everything that we do. For the most part we manage to push it to the backs of our minds; the young are oblivious to it; the middle-aged think it may never happen; the old fear it. But throughout life we are jockeying for position in relation to a competitive structure where survival for as long as possible and avoidance of death (usually) for as long as possible are our principal aims. And therefore death shapes life.

If 'In the midst of life we are in death' in the magnificent words of the Prayer Book funeral service – and who could deny it? – ought we to fear death? Is it not a crime against the Christian faith to fear death? If God has deemed it necessary and right to use death as the means to bring about his purposes in the universe – the death of everything from the amoeba to the blue whale – why should we view death as something terrible or 'obscene' (as I put it just now), a curse inflicted upon creation in response to primordial sin?

I think that the answer is because we look upon death as the termination of a process which is not yet complete. We struggle against death, clinging to life, and in so doing we distort the shape of our lives. We know that we have (accidents excepted) between seventy and eighty years on this earth, yet somehow we want more. Why? What makes us think that if we have not reached our goal in seventy years we shall somehow manage it in seven hundred? What makes us think that if we have been at a loss to know what to do with seventy years we shall reasonably solve the problem of what to do with seven hundred years or even with everlasting life in heaven with God?

What about Evolution?

Some would cut all these difficulties away by choosing to dispense with evolutionary theory altogether, returning to Adam and Eve in the Garden of Eden, and to sin as that which is the source of all death as a result of the curse imposed upon humankind lest they should 'live for ever' (Genesis 3.22). Here, disobedience is held up as the source of our plight, just as it is in much of the Old Testament. The Israelites disobeyed God time and time again, and each time they were punished. Death is represented as a consequence of sin. Death is 'the last enemy' (I Corinthians 15.26) because death arises from sin, and because sin is also the enemy that corrupts and destroys humankind's existence before God, breaking the bonds between them and introducing an infinitely deep gulf that we cannot cross.

This is traditional Hebrew, Jewish and Christian teaching. According to Genesis 2 and 3, first there was law ('you must not eat from the tree of the knowledge of good and evil'); then there was disobedience ('the serpent deceived me and I ate'); then there was guilt ('they realised that they were naked, so they sewed fig-leaves together'); then there was discovery and punishment ('with pain you will give birth to children'); and lastly there was exile from paradise, 'and a flaming sword flashing back and forth to guard the way to the tree of life'.

Magnificent! But wildly misleading, of course, if seen either as history or as biology. This passage is a product of the mind of a Hebrew writer of sheer poetic genius and deep religious insight. But there has always been death; evolution depends upon it. There has never been a paradise; we climbed from the primaeval slime (but such wonderfully rich slime, pregnant with possibilities beyond number). There were false starts, aborted strains (the dinosaurs the most magnificent dead end), faltering planets, new births and sudden deaths along the way.

Evolutionary biology repeatedly criticizes accounts of the involvement of God in the development of worlds and species by pointing out that every change that has ever occurred in any species can, with certain gaps yet to be filled, be explained in terms of natural selection and random genetic mutation.

One wonders how often biologists need to be shown that this argument is completely irrelevant to the question of divine involvement. Their argument involves repeatedly making a very simple logical error. We cannot predict the future because we cannot predict the long-term effects of random changes that have not yet taken place. But when we look at the past, those changes have taken place, and we can see what they were. 'This happened' (by chance) then 'that happened' (by chance) and so on. But biologists' preference for making chance an absolute here is nothing but blind prejudice. No argument they can use shows that God *could not* have been involved in selecting which random mutations should occur; it is simply that they choose to assert that God *need not* or *did not* have such a role. Accounts of evolution which attribute the emergence of species to God's creative influence are, therefore, immune to scientific criticism. And the same applies on logical grounds to God's potential involvement in the future of the world. To prove that God could not possibly have acted in a given circumstance we would need to have under our control every variable that might affect that circumstance, and to be able to detect the deviation of any variable from the value it would normally take. In other words, we would need to be able to say what would or might have happened. This we can simply never do. Such knowledge and control are not merely practically very difficult; they are theoretically impossible. This is the essence of Stephen Hawking's argument to the effect that the future is intrinsically indeterminate. God has made the world to rely upon the throws of countless 'dice', while reserving for himself opportunities to cheat.

Of course, there may be life on other worlds. What kind of a God do we believe in to wish to deny it? But that life too will be compassed about by death; that life too will endure pain and suffer mental anguish (to the extent that it has risen to a level of complexity sufficient to conceive anguish). What is the problem? It is this: If there is life on other worlds, how can God only have become incarnate on this world, or even have become incarnate exclusively on any world at all? How, in other words, can Jesus of Nazareth, the man from Galilee, have significance for the whole universe?

What about Jesus (Again)?

This is to see things upside-down. It involves still thinking of Jesus as someone whose significance and importance lies in the fact that we believe in him, and so we conclude that if there is life on other worlds (life which self-evidently cannot believe in him), either God must have become incarnate on those worlds too, or God did not become incarnate on this one.

To think this is to have missed the point. Jesus is not there so that we can believe in him; he is not there so that we can come to know God; he is not even there so that we can come to know what it is like to be God. He is there so that God can come to know what it is like to be us. Jesus is God's way to find out what it is like to be one of his own creatures (first and foremost), and only then (and in a thoroughly secondary sense) an opportunity for God's creatures to know what God is like.

The problem just raised (of life on other worlds being ignorant of Jesus) is no different from the problem of those who live and die on this world in complete ignorance of Jesus (because they lived before he was born, or in the jungle where nobody told them, or in a part of the world where they were given no opportunity to hear about him or believe in him). So if life on other worlds 'cannot be saved' without an incarnation on those worlds, neither can the vast majority of humankind.

The salvation which Jesus secures is not dependent on anyone knowing about it, believing in it, or hearing the Good News. The salvation Jesus secures is secured because in Jesus God comes to know what it is like to be a creature, and is therefore enabled to judge creatures from a position of equality with them. Jesus, whom we declare to be 'Our Judge' is such because in Jesus God finds out about the stresses and strains, the temptations and opportunities of life as a creature in the universe, and is therefore in a position to make a reasonable and just assessment of what we should and should not, can and cannot, could and could not do with our lives. In Jesus God comes to know the secrets of our hearts as we know the secrets of one another's hearts, and he judges us in that light.

None of us is exempt from the knowledge of our innermost selves that comes to another human being who meets us. And so we are all known by Jesus as we know one another, but even more deeply. God became man in order that he might know us as we know ourselves, and so judge us as such. It is not a matter of whether we know him yet, or whether he knows us, but that one day we will all know him and be known by him in the person of Jesus, the Son of God. And in the sounding of that knell we find ourselves called to heaven or to hell (*Macbeth*).

All this talk of life on other worlds, of the life in this world that never hears about Jesus or God or anything to bring it into contact with the source of the universe, seems to raise serious questions about what God was doing when he created the universe.

What about Creation?

Where once we had Genesis chapter one and God saying, 'Let there be light!' we now have the Big Bang, an expanding universe, curved space-time, quarks, general relativity and quantum mechanics. But has anything really changed? I think not.

There is nothing in modern theories of the cosmos to contradict the idea that the universe exists because a Supreme Being (albeit one of limited powers) brought it into existence. Physicists, of course, pretend to have burrowed to the bottom of the cosmic heap and found a vacuum capable of bringing the universe out of nothing through quantum fluctuations. This, of course, is complete nonsense. Absolute nothing has no physics. The kind of 'nothing' physicists talk about when they talk of the quantum void is positively teeming with qualities that absolute nothing cannot have. Absolute nothing has no qualities. That is why it is absolute. And nothing.

Of course, 'explanations' of the universe that appeal to God no more provide final explanations than explanations in terms of quantum fluctuations in the void. The question, 'Where did God come from?' is scarcely answered by saying that God has existed forever (a forever stretching back even before created time). It is very much a matter of, 'You pays your money and you takes your choice'. I have given an account in earlier sections of my own convictions and why I hold them.

The person of Jesus is the beginning of all things, the central pivot upon which all truth turns. I understand everything else in relation to this truth, and this truth is the Incarnation of the Word who was in the beginning with God, and by whom all things were made. Nothing else troubles me. But if I bring in the connection between Jesus, the Incarnate Word, the Word who was in the beginning with God, and the creation of the world, Christians may want to ask a supplementary question about the relationship between God and Jesus. This, together with the problem of the place of the Holy Spirit, is a question about the Trinity.

What about the Trinity?

Christians think that the Trinity is very difficult to understand. I have some sympathy with them, for the Trinity is often 'explained' in terms of models and analogies (a lot of them invented by St Augustine) that are profoundly misleading and excessively complicated.

I would like to try to start again and give my own very simple account (which is very much the account we find in Karl Barth, but with the technical bits removed).

There is an aspect of God whom we can never know as such since this God lies beyond anything that created beings could ever understand. Call this God the Father.

There is an aspect of God whom we can know, whom some of us do know, and whom we encounter in a human being called Jesus of Nazareth. Call this God the Son.

There is an aspect of God through whom we encounter God in others and in the world, but indirectly, in that we encounter others and the world exactly as they are (as John Puddefoot or a tree or a cow) but in and through our encounter with them we find ourselves encountering God. Call this God the Holy Spirit.

The whole business is made much more difficult when we ask about what it is like to be a triune God. I think we should just refuse to ask such an impertinent question. It is enough that we know God in Jesus and through the Holy Spirit. Let us leave God as he knows himself to God.

One thing I do wonder about God as he knows himself is whether perhaps he does not know himself any more fully and completely than we do (that is what I would call 'the image of God in humankind'). Perhaps, just as we are constantly discovering things about ourselves and our potential by speaking new words and performing new actions, so God may learn new things about himself as he creates and sustains the world (while all the time no doubt being engaged in lots of other activities we cannot begin to think of, let alone comprehend).

(The other thing I know about God is that he is not male, that calling God 'he' is deeply problematic, and that I shouldn't do it. But I think 'she' would be equally ridiculous, 'it' would be an insult, and 'Godself' is a barbarism, so I hope that even the feminists will allow me this piece of political incorrectness.)

But I have so far given insufficient attention to the so-called Third person of the Trinity, and yet in many ways from our point of view (between the 'no longer' of the resurrection and ascension and the 'not yet' of the end of the world) he is the most important.

What about the Holy Spirit?

In what I have said so far I may inadvertently have given the impression that I take account, in the final analysis, only of myself and Jesus. This would be a major (if understandable) misreading of the situation.

When I encounter someone, I am conscious that whatever their beliefs, they may deliberately or, more likely, inadvertently, be a vehicle for God's revelation. It is not necessary for them to try self-consciously to be such a vehicle; God may use their words and actions in his service whether they like it or not.

But they should not be too offended. God may equally use the moon and the stars in the same way, and what is really happening is that his presence in the world here and now is somehow presenting itself to me. This is the work of the Holy Spirit. The Holy Spirit is God's presence in the world, the aspect of God who is present in the world.

So if I am listening to a sermon, or attending a Eucharist, or saying a prayer, or reading a book, or talking to someone, or fast asleep, or sitting at my computer typing these words, and I have a thought which I deem worthy of attributing to God (I can never be sure of that, of course), it is to the work of God as Holy Spirit that I attribute the action that produced that thought in me. The same holds true when I read the Bible, or hear the Bible read, or read the Church Fathers, or even (unlikely as it may seem) if I am reading something completely secular like Shakespeare or Stendhal or George Eliot or Rainer Maria Rilke, and something I deem worthy of attribution to God comes into my mind.

Something absolutely central and vital is at stake here: that God is alive; that God not only may be, but actually must be present if human words are to convey the divine Word. That unless God reads the book, their labour is but lost that read it; that unless God protects the city, the watchmen wake in vain.

As we saw in the case of the Bible, it is not the nature of the text that makes the book special or holy, but the way in which the text is read. If we are to discover those aspects of ourselves which we can only have access to when we find ourselves in the presence of God (compare my story of the contemplative nuns), God must be actively present in that process.

I am trying to give an impression of what it is to live one's life with a living God who makes everything one does into something different from what it would be were he to be absent from that action, and who makes every word mean differently from what it would mean were he absent from the reading of it. I hope that it is unnecessary to say that I do not pretend to have come anywhere near to achieving that sense of God's presence in my own life. But I do hope that in putting things this way I may help others to make a better job of it than I can.

The Bible is not the Word of God, but in the power of God the Holy Spirit it has the capacity (but not the unique capacity) to *become* the Word of God. Whatever we read has no power of itself to convey God's Word. The Anglican expostulation at the end of the public reading of Scripture, 'This is the Word of the Lord!' is very misleading. It may become the Word of the Lord, but it is not and cannot be of itself the Word of the Lord.

But does that not involve a terrible ambiguity? If we believe that God must be present to interpret all that we say and do, how can we ever be sure that what we say and do is of God and not merely of ourselves?

What about Freedom?

The principal result of this reawakening of a sense of the presence of God as Holy Spirit in all that we do (if what we do is to become something in which God can act or make himself known) is to convince us of the wonderful freedom before God that we enjoy.

For much of my early life I experienced Christianity as a

strait-jacket, a constricting, limiting, rigid set of beliefs held in fear lest I should find myself punished by God. I have spent much of the last twenty years ridding myself of all the accumulated nonsense and rubbish of that early life. If I seem at times to have been harsh, it is because my own memories reveal to me how great can be the oppressiveness of a religion adhered to in fear, and because having rid myself of such fear I can now rejoice in the freedom that comes from a vision of the glory of God.

The principal freedoms that I feel when I think about what I do and do not believe are twofold: a freedom *from* any requirement to satisfy, obey, or pay lip-service to the trappings, services and processes of organized, institutional religion, including any sense of restriction on what I may or may not read, do or say, those with whom I may or may not consort, meet and mingle; and a freedom *for* the rich variety of human life in all its forms, including its glories and its shame.

We find both these kinds of emphasis in Jesus' teachings and life. Consider, 'The Sabbath was made for man, not man for the Sabbath' (Mark 2.27) or, 'What goes into a man's mouth does not make him "unclean", but what comes out of his mouth, that is what makes him "unclean"' (Matthew 15.11). In consorting with the social and religious outcasts of his day, his life embodied his teaching: we are not made unclean by reaching out to tax-gatherers, prostitutes, lepers and madmen. We should rather hunger and thirst after righteousness, for the bread which comes down from heaven and gives life to the world.

We should abandon for ever any practices, hopes or dreams designed to secure or centred upon questions of our own salvation. Yet many religious people still see religion as a way to control what we touch and whom we meet (to ensure that they are, and we remain, clean). For them, entering into a place where one might be corrupted is as bad as being corrupted; speaking to a sinner (the New Testament singles out prostitutes and tax-gatherers as typical social outcasts in this respect) is in itself corrupting; it makes us ritually unclean. But that is quite contrary to Jesus' teaching that it is what comes out of us which matters. Neither must this be read solely in terms of Jewish laws of cleanliness; religions of all kinds tend to set up boundaries which protect their members from contamination by contact with certain 'undesirables'. The matter is particularly clear in questions of sexual behaviour, where most religions hold virginity in high regard because it is a state of purity, and similarly regard celibacy, continence and self-denial as more virtuous than any kind of sexual intimacy. That is one reason why prostitution has always been singled out for special condemnation, and why some (but by no means all) religious people find such things as Aids so difficult to come to terms with.

Christ's followers should be above such petty considerations as are involved in these matters of social cleanliness. Not because they are more or less corruptible or incorruptible, further above or below temptation, more or less immune to the things that sully the soul, than 'other human beings', but because they are persuaded that the love of God made known in Christ Jesus is not there to be taken away, and that the last person on earth for whom I ought to have any concern is myself.

What about Morality?

Quite obviously, such freedom presents us with temptations. To abandon concern for oneself because one has seen the glory of God made known in the love of Jesus could easily become a licence to do exactly as one pleased, a chronic perversion of St Paul's ironic question, 'Shall we go on sinning, so that grace may increase?' (Romans 6.1). But I am more deeply concerned about another aspect of morality that is closely akin to the questions we have already addressed about belief and worship.

There are, no doubt, those who adopt a moral lifestyle because they fear that if they do not they will be punished by God (just as there are those who profess to believe in God, and those who regularly worship God, for fear of what might happen were they to do otherwise). No doubt the world is a better place because there are such people, for it would be a terrible place were we all murderers and villains with no moral sense at all. But even if fear is better than nothing, can a genuine moral sense be based upon it? A morality based upon fear of what may happen to us if we fail to do what God requires may lack any coherent structure. For example, believing that right belief governs salvation has led us to do all sorts of things (such as burn those we consider to be heretics) which are, on the face of it, deeply immoral.

So moral behaviour adopted out of fear by following rules becomes a substitute for moral behaviour that arises spontaneously from a living relationship with a living God. We imagine that we are doing what God wants on the basis of our obedience to commandments that were written thousands of years ago. What if circumstances change, and the situation that obtained thousands of years ago is not the same as the situation in which we find ourselves?

The trouble, as has so frequently been observed by those who have thought about these matters, is that the Bible just does not give us clear guidance on questions such as abortion, euthanasia, *in vitro* fertilization, surrogate motherhood, embryo research, genetic engineering and all the other things that are currently of concern to us as our technology advances ahead of a moral theory to guide it.

In my view, the reason why we lack an adequate response to such moral dilemmas is that we have placed too much reliance upon historic text such as the Bible, and upon moral principles stated in doctrine, and not enough upon a relationship with the living God. Yet if God is not alive and able to guide us, he is dead, and there seems little point in believing in a Bible which purports to tell us the views of a God who is dead, or is travelling, or 'Maybe is sleeping' (1 Kings 18.27).

So, if we are to discover answers to moral dilemmas that are not discussed either in the Bible or in the historic teachings of the Church, we need to understand how to place ourselves in God's presence and to converse with God about what we should do. To put the matter that way makes it seem very difficult, even implausible, but what other answer can we give if the God we believe in is alive?

The real problem is that our moral views are muddled with social and political concerns, personal fears and anxieties, and taboos which have lost their original reasons for existing. Absolute moral teachings presuppose that the same answer will do in every circumstance, and that an absolute God requires us all to act in the same way in all conceivable circumstances. I very seriously doubt whether such a view is sustainable, and so I come to another radical suggestion: there may be different right actions in different circumstances; some of those right actions may appear to contradict one another.

What about Consistency?

As children of a scientific age, we like the idea of universal laws which can be printed on a T-shirt, and which cover every conceivable case that could arise throughout the universe. I am personally not at all convinced that such laws exist, because I think they are 'purchased' at the expense of ignoring the specific and unique content of each individual event they seek to model, but that is not the point at issue here.

The ideal of universal, scientific, natural law suggests a corresponding ideal of a universal moral law. Such a universal moral law seems to fit with our ideas of God. God knows the difference between right and wrong; that knowledge is absolute; therefore there is an absolute difference between right and wrong.

The logic is flawed. God in his wisdom may well know the right thing we should do here, but that does not (as far as I can see) require us to do the same thing there where circumstances are slightly different. You, in your life, and at your stage of life, with your commitments and responsibilities, may be in a position – for example – where it is right for you to divorce your husband or wife. I, in my circumstances and with my commitments and responsibilities, with apparently equal cause (let us suppose each of our spouses has committed adultery), may be equally wrong to divorce. The idea that divorce is absolutely either right or wrong (as has been maintained for most of human history and is still taught by the Roman Catholic Church) is one which actually makes little sense once we accept that no two circumstances are ever the same.

This is what I meant in the previous section about our moral views being muddled with social and political concerns. It is convenient to have universal moral laws because they enable us to decide easily what is right and what is wrong. We can apply a simple set of rules to any circumstances. If divorce is wrong, requests for divorce can be dealt with instantly and without even hearing the details of the case. In practice, we have never been able to sustain such a hard-headed line. It has always been necessary to consider the circumstances. There have always been exceptions. But the backdrop to our concern has always been the fear that widespread divorce would produce massive social dislocation, such as problems with delinquent children who do not know who or where both parents are.

And at the root of our objections to the suggestion that there are in fact different circumstances to be taken into account where each moral decision has to be made is the fear that it will be impossible to police such a variable set of considerations. How can we possibly know in every conceivable circumstance what is right and what is wrong?

This same concern surrounds the problem of a Christian ethical theory that is based upon the relationship between an individual believer and God. Once we abandon belief in absolute moral norms we seem to be granting each individual *carte blanche* to do as he or she likes. Moral chaos seems to loom over the horizon.

This is, once again, really the same kind of argument as St Paul's ironic, 'Shall we go on sinning, so that grace may increase?' (Romans 6.1) To suggest that someone deeply concerned to commune with the living God and to direct his or her life on the basis of that communion would deceive us into thinking that God had directed him or her this way when in truth he had directed him or her that way, is just not credible. Nobody who had a relationship with God of the kind we have been discussing would do such a thing. The 'Let us go on sinning, so that grace may increase' argument only works if those concerned have no idea what grace is, and the concern we express about our capacity to direct our lives guided by God is only real if we do not believe in the possibility of a relationship with God of sufficient intimacy to permit it.

In other words, a desire for an easy-to-administer absolute moral law that takes little or no account of personal circumstances and denies the rights of individuals to direct their own lives 'following the commandments of God' as the Prayer Book puts it, is a child of unbelief. It amounts to a desire for a rule-book that covers every eventuality. Such rules could be applied quite independently of a real, living relationship with God or our neighbour. They would remove the need for a living faith, adapting to the peculiarities of human circumstance and exhibiting human compassion under the guidance of God. In this sense an absolute moral law is a child of unbelief, something we would only need if God were dead.

How does this argument stand in relation to doctrine?

What about Doctrine?

What is Christian doctrine? It is the product of the distilled reflection and wisdom of those concerned with the relationship between human beings and God over two thousand years. As such it is not final, inviolate, fixed in concrete and infallible. Those who seek to make doctrine or church pronouncements 'infallible' are clutching at straws. Doctrine is to theology what scaffolding is to a building: it is there to help us along, not to replace that which it helps us to build and repair.

Unfortunately, doctrine is often confused with dogma, and dogma amounts (in most minds) to dictatorial insistence upon certain truths regardless of whether and to what extent they are rational or justifiable. We fall back upon dogma when reason fails, as in the well-known margin note to a weak sermon: 'Argument thin; shout louder!' Dogmatism is the theological equivalent of stamping one's foot. But if we see doctrine in terms of scaffolding, a help towards greater things rather than the things themselves, we shall approach it with a more constructive frame of mind.

Doctrine teaches us the kinds of things that others have found it profitable to think, affirm and believe. It should not be regarded as a necessary precondition for entry into heaven (as if St Peter administered a test on Christian doctrine before admitting anyone through the heavenly gates). And doctrine, like the Scriptures, is fallible, changeable, imperfect.

In the end, we make our own decisions about how we will live our lives. We choose on the basis of deep feelings, resonances, hopes and fears, as well as loves and hates. But above all we choose on the basis of the kind of person we are and the kind of person we wish to become.

And the same goes for those doctrines we are prepared to believe. Where we are still thinking of Christian believing in terms of willingness to tick a long series of boxes alongside statements of faith, doctrines assume an importance they do not deserve. They become burdens which torture our intellect and threaten to tear apart the unity of our beliefs. Those we feel we have to accept despite the fact that we deem them unreasonable or irrational (some would cite the Virgin Birth in this context, although I do not myself have a problem with it) make us feel deeply uncomfortable. They also reinforce the sense in which we believe not for the sake of today and the enrichment of our present physical, mental and spiritual lives, but in order to try to make sure that we have earned everlasting life by adhering to the required list of teachings.

We should turn the whole matter round, make doctrines guidelines for fruitful ideas to ponder, helping hands along the path to a deeper faith. We will then no longer be frightened by intense, searching questions such as are so often asked by those fired with evangelical zeal: 'Do you believe in the Virgin Birth?'; 'Do you believe Jesus calmed the storm?'; 'Do you believe Jesus raised Lazarus?' and so forth (which make belief appear like a series of hoops we have to jump through in order to be acceptable – but acceptable to whom?) Where a doctrine does not point us in a direction in which we feel able to go, there we find ourselves unable to glean such insights as it offers us. But that is to our disadvantage; it hampers (usually in only a minor way) our maturity in the faith. It does not put at risk the salvation of our immortal souls (whatever the fundamentalist may say to the contrary).

But we stand in need of one further source of guidance if we are not to be left utterly to ourselves and the excesses of individual whim. We need the wisdom and the guidance of others, and that leads us, in the Christian context, to ask yet another question.

What about the Church?

The Church, in sharp contrast to the various churches that are in evidence about the world, is simply the set of all the places and events in the world where God the Holy Spirit is active and is discerned. As such it is the place on earth where God is encountered and known. The Church so conceived is sharply to be distinguished from any institution which calls itself a church or 'the' church. The Church is not subject to human jurisdiction; 'the Spirit blows wherever it pleases' (John 3.8).

That we can be members of this Church regardless of our allegiance to any institutional form of the Christian religion is a source of endless embarrassment to those who run the institutional churches. Their need to control the churches is so great that they are prepared to attempt to set limits to what God can do in order to say what is and is not a revelation of God.

We should deny them this right. The Spirit blows where it wills, and God will reveal himself where God wills, without fear of any church injunction. Whatever the churches may seek to achieve, God will never allow the Church in the power of the Spirit to become the Spirit in the power of the churches. Just as he kept seven thousand in Israel who had not bowed the knee to Ba'al (1 Kings 19.18; Romans 11.4), so he is able of the stones to raise up children for Abraham (Matthew 3.9). The true Church will never be determined by human whim, desire or institutional canon.

The force of this claim is apparent from the central Jewish and Christian idea of God pouring out his Spirit 'on all people' (Joel 2.28) in such a way that the notion of the need for some third party to stand between human beings and God - priests or churches - is done away with. Both through the baptism of the Holy Spirit at Pentecost, which empowered the disciples to preach in God's name, and in our own lives, God has given us direct access to himself through Jesus Christ in the power of the Spirit. It is that gift which no institutional edict can take away, for, much to some parts of the institution's chagrin, that gift comes from God. The churches have taken various steps to try to circumscribe this gift at different times, for example by making sacraments the means whereby grace is given, or ordination the one source of spiritual authority, or theological erudition a criterion for preaching and teaching. But note the devastating impact of the view expressed in Hebrews 8.11 in this context: 'No longer will a man teach his neighbour, or a man his brother, saying, "Know the Lord" because they will all know me, from the least of them to the greatest' quoting Jeremiah 31.31-35).

What about Prayer?

Because Christianity dispenses with intermediaries with its doctrine of the one priesthood of Jesus Christ and the outpouring of the Holy Spirit on all flesh, the most central action of the Christian is prayer. Yet even if prayer is the most practised Christian action, it is also perhaps the least understood and the most abused of the activities in which Christians engage. It seems to be something which we do naturally as human beings, and we commonly speak of praying for something to happen even in contexts which are not religious. The football manager 'prays' for a goal (which just means 'hopes fervently' for one); we 'pray' for rain (which just means we 'are desperate' for it). but we also 'pray to God'. What does that mean?

These everyday uses spill over into religious prayer, where we often find ourselves asking God for things such as 'a safe journey' or 'relief from sickness'. Jews, at least in some of their traditions, are much better at praying than Christians. There is a tradition of openness and honesty in Jewish prayer – that if we think God has left us in the lurch, we tell him so in no uncertain terms – which is altogether lost in the mealy-mouthed prayers of Christians. They seem to feel that being honest with God with their lips is not permissible (however great the anguish in their hearts), and that unless their prayers begin by telling God how wonderful he is and how unworthy we are, they are not likely to work.

The meaning of prayer can only be understood within the context of the change that takes place in us when we find ourselves near to God. That does not mean, of course, that God is otherwise far away; it simply means that we are changed when we are aware of him (just as we are changed when we are near certain people and in certain places). We pray publicly and we pray in private; we pray for things and we pray to focus our minds. So there are four mixtures of these ways of praying: public intercession, public focus, private intercession and private focus.

PUBLIC INTERCESSION

One of the most helpful things I have heard said about public prayer I owe to John Polkinghorne, who drew an analogy in his book *Science and Providence* (SPCK 1989) between the focus of public prayer and a laser beam. A laser beam is a beam of light of considerable intensity. All the light is of the same wavelength or 'colour', and so it is very precise. By bringing the light together in this way (the beam generates the light to be of the same wavelength by a kind of self-reproducing physical process which is focused by the apparatus) it assumes a purity which means that it can be targeted very accurately.

Public intercession is best thought of by analogy with this as a way to focus the corporate mind of the congregation upon one concern. I do not myself believe for a moment that the effect of all these people praying for the same thing is to 'twist God's arm' into doing something, but I do believe that this kind of corporate focus gives the problem a vividness and intensity which serves to make us more ready to do something about it ourselves. It so-to-speak sensitizes us to something. Of course, in some congregations nothing much happens, but occasionally an individual or a small group of people will be empowered by this kind of focus to take action, or lives may be changed.

This way of looking at prayer is to make it a purely social, even psychological phenomenon. What does such corporate prayer do to God? Is God persuaded to do something differently because enough of his children demand that he does so? The honest answer to such a question must be, 'Who knows?' For myself, the only occasion upon which I feel that public intercession has any real purpose (rather than being no more than an attempt to persuade God to do things we are too lazy or indifferent to do ourselves) is when we have our backs to the wall and, despite having employed our best efforts, have failed to achieve what needed to be achieved. Then I think coming before the Lord with our burdens upon our hearts has more of a ring of truth to it, and may by that very token be more likely to evoke God's compassion. (But I am sure that there have been countless instances in human history where even this has proved a delusion, and so I am reluctant to make much of it.)

PUBLIC FOCUS

In other kinds of public prayer I think it very doubtful whether we have any expectation at all that anything will 'happen' or that God will 'do anything'. Prayers for the State, the Royal Family, the ministry of the Church, and so forth, seem much more a matter of corporate focus. By praying in the presence of God (as we think and intend) and voicing these thoughts and hopes, we cement our community identity behind a certain expression of concern. Such prayer, naturally present in an established church such as the Church of England, serves to underline the connections between individuals and the structures of Church and State.

The laser beam analogy still seems to have some mileage in it even here. Little more may happen than that we are reminded occasionally that we are all part of a larger group with common interests and concerns, and that the nation as a whole owes certain kinds of loyalty to certain institutions. (This remains generally true whether or not we approve of the Royal Family, the particular government that is in power, or the local clergy.)

Yet this again makes public prayer largely a matter of social, even sociological importance, and little else. But this objection betrays a lingering obsession with doing what we believe God would have us do. Somehow we imagine that God listens to our prayers more readily when they are voiced corporately, by clergymen, in public worship, and that the secrets of the heart (which Jesus tells us are known even before we utter them) somehow fall otherwise on deaf divine ears.

And it is always interesting to reflect on the extent to which, during the last two thousand years, we have chosen which of Jesus' injunctions to take seriously and which quietly to forget.

PRIVATE INTERCESSION

When we come to private intercession we also come to hopes, thoughts and requests that tend to be much more precise. But how much do we genuinely believe God is willing or able to do as a result of such prayer? Is it conceivable, for instance, that a loving God able to do something to help us would fail to do so simply because we had not asked for it?

Speaking for myself, I have to admit that I have grown less and less inclined to private intercessory prayer as a result of this argument. I do not believe, as many believe, that God interferes with the course of the world at the drop of a hat just because I or someone else happens to need some small 'favour' to ease some burden or smooth some passage through life. Part of God's wisdom can be seen in the way that he leaves us in almost all circumstances to run our own lives.

When we come to prayers arising from fear and anguish, I have further doubts to share. They may well make us feel better, but I do not for a moment believe (in almost all circumstances) that they have any actual effect. For example, I once flew to New Zealand for a conference. We were coming in to land at Wellington airport, and, as is common there, the winds were high and the aeroplane was swinging about alarmingly during its approach. I noticed that several passengers sitting around me had their eyes closed, and one had his hands clasped together, apparently in prayer. I found myself both unable and unwilling to join him. It struck me then as it strikes me now (and as it struck me with considerably more force years earlier when I faced a relatively serious kidney operation) that prayer was completely pointless in such circumstances. God's will is simply that the world will do what the world does. I have no expectation that God will intervene to stop my plane from crashing or the surgeon's knife from slipping.

But I am not completely sceptical. I am persuaded by the story of the judge who eventually gives the woman what she wants to stop her pestering him (Luke 18.1–8) that there are occasional circumstances in which we may in fact influence God to act. I see this as an element in a partnership between God and his creatures that is permitted because the future of the world is not fixed in advance, and therefore open to direction. My only hesitation arises from the possibility – which some will find even more worrying than my doubts about the general effectiveness of intercessory prayer – that by persuading God to act as we deem necessary, we may actually make matters worse than they would have been had he not acted. A wise old woman, now long dead, whom I knew when I was a curate, once put it this way: 'Be careful what you pray for; your prayer may be answered.'

PRIVATE FOCUS

I come finally to the most important kind of prayer. In private meditation we explore the deepest thoughts of our own hearts in openness and holiness before God, 'coming before the Lord bearing our burdens upon our heart' as the late great Michael Ramsay once put it. This is not the place for a detailed discussion of how such prayer is to be entered into, but two remarks are in order.

First, the presence of God in our hearts and minds is often indistinguishable from our own thoughts and feelings, longings and emotions. We simply cannot say 'this came from God' and 'this came from me' as if God's Word as it manifests itself in our minds had a label like Paddington Bear saying 'from highest heaven' (rather than 'from darkest Peru'). God's Word is always also our own word, just as the Bible is both our own (fallible) words as well as having the power to become God's Word. Therefore meditative prayer consists primarily in listening to ourselves and, by listening intently to ourselves, learning to see what we should do with our lives.

Second, meditative prayer is central to all religious life. Through it the thoughts which allow us to understand the whole universe come to us. We lose all sense of any difference between God 'out there' and God 'in here', between what is commonly called God's transcendence and God's immanence, by learning that however and wherever God is present in the world, we can only see him there by allowing the presence of God in our own hearts and minds – our own deepest selves – to show us that he is there.

If we look at a sunset, at the great dome of stars in the night sky, at a landscape, at a slum, at a dying child, and we can see the presence of God in each in different ways, it is not because there is something out there with a label on it saying 'this comes from God', but because we have in our deepest selves a divine presence which interprets what we see and shows us where God is to be found.

I am sure that this is what Bishop John Robinson meant by 'the beyond in the midst' when he wrote *Honest to God* (SCM 1963), and what he rather unwisely and regrettably allowed to dissolve into an apparent denial that there is an independent 'other' God at all. There is most emphatically an 'other' God, a God who would exist though heaven and earth were to pass away – let there be no misunderstanding on this point – but, if we are to be able to see and hear and know and experience this 'other' God, we must learn to encounter him, and to have our lives directed and interpreted by him, by finding him in the irruption of our deepest selves in the meditation of private prayer.

This God is the 'intrascendent' God, the beyond in the midst, the God who although over and above all is also only known by being present and by interpreting all things within (intra-) each individual heart.

What about Revelation?

There will be those who will object to the way I intend to express the realization of God's presence by discovering who I am and being put in touch with that self which echoes most fully to the being of God. They will say that 'I am who I am' is the name God gave to himself (see Exodus 3.14), and that it is not for us to take that name for ourselves. My reply, apart from making the rueful observation that someone who objected to that would probably have given up on this book some time ago, would be to deny that in the end we can ever experience God other than in ourselves.

This is really a trivial point, but it seems to cause offence. We want somehow to know the God 'out there' quite independently of ourselves. It is as if to know God in ourselves is to soil God with ourselves. It is as if we want to keep God clean and distant. But a moment's reflection is enough to show that everything we know, we know in ourselves. Our bodies are clever enough to treat our knowledge as if it were of the real exterior world, but all our sensations of that world occur in our heads. God is certainly 'other' and 'out there'. So is the table at which I type. But I know both of them 'in here', inside my self – trivially. And I measure the adequacy of my knowledge of them by the effects they have on me. And it is equally true that what we know of God we learn from 'out there' as well as from inside ourselves, from other human beings, from the natural world, from the Bible. But in the end it is our own knowing, and it takes place inside each of us.

This inner knowing is particularly important in the case of God. Unlike the table, where if I understand it wrongly I may bump into it, bruise my shins, and knock it over, spilling coffee cups all over the floor, I cannot 'test' my knowledge of God on physical objects in the world. The only tests I can use are those that come from the community of believers (what they teach me and how they respond to what I try to teach them), and from my own deepest self. I test my nearness to God in terms of becoming that self I most fully am, and I sense that by the feeling of rightness associated with harmony between myself, my neighbours, and my God.

What about Spirituality?

I would like to conclude with an extended meditation on the way in which God may reveal himself through human beings and the way in which our attitude to God's revelation defines our being. Through it, the way human beings may experience the revelation of God in themselves is illustrated. It should be read in the light of what has been said in the remainder of the book, and especially what was said in the previous section. In God, I am what I am, and I will become what I can most fully be.

As a small crumb of comfort and consolation to those who have endured my political incorrectness thus far, I attribute my story to a female, whom we shall call Louise. (For further discussion of the Inside/Outside distinction, see my *God and the Mind Machine*, SPCK 1996.)

THE OUTSIDE STORY

Let us suppose that someone strikes us as so utterly remarkable through her words and actions that we begin to consider the possibility that God is present in her to an unusual extent. We put this suggestion to her, but she denies any sense of that presence, any consciousness of ever having had a religious experience. We cross-examine her about what it is, in that case, which fuels and inspires her words and actions: from what source does she draw her wisdom and strength? Her only answer, the only answer she is able to give that seems to her to come anywhere near to explaining these powers (powers which she is at some pains to play down), is that much of her life has been given over to consideration of the question of the nature of God, to study of what others have written of God and done in God's name, and to her own attempts not so much to imitate others as to find a way to live her own life that resonates at a deep and inarticulate level with what she feels herself to be, to be called to be and to need to be.

Most of us, I think, would be impressed by this as a description of what it is to try to live a life guided by God, but we might equally be dissatisfied with how small a part her awareness of God's presence and guidance seemed to play in executing that process. When pressed, she denies again any sense of the presence of God at all; all she will acknowledge is the presence of a vast array of thoughts about God gleaned from the sayings and writings and lives of others. She does admit, however, that even if she were able to list all these words, they would not be sufficient to afford us a complete account of her life or how she lives it.

We ask what else we would need to know. She replies that just as when we use words, even in the most humdrum and everyday contexts, our words spring from a deep well of desires, intentions and dreams, but nevertheless give expression to our selves, so her words and actions – the way she lives her life – spring from something she calls her deepest self. That self is more than the words she speaks and the acts she performs; it gives birth to those words and actions, it manifests itself through them, it throw itself into a communicable form in them, but it is not and cannot be identified with them.

When we do not entirely see what she is getting at, she continues by pointing out that this reservoir she calls her deepest self has been filled by the streams of thoughts, words and actions she has studied, experienced, valued, searched after. But she also says that it is a mere prejudice of our time to suppose that we could ever give a complete account of all these streams (reducing them to strings of bits of information, as the cybernetics industry seeks to do, that could be programmed into a computer), and an even greater prejudice to suppose that there can be no other influences upon a human being than those which are found in the things of the world. To the extent that she will admit to the presence of God in her life at all, she insists that it is more likely to be apparent to others through her words and actions, through their discernment of God's presence in her, than something she is conscious of herself. She argues strenuously and somewhat aggressively that the idea that experiences of God are accessible to introspection cannot be ruled out, but that it is another facet of our western individualism to try to make experience of God a possession, something we can each enjoy in ourselves, and that this strand of individualism tempts us to seek religious experiences for their own sake.

What motivates her is the quest for fullness of life, fulfilment of her own gifts, her own capacity to be what she is capable of being. She cannot conceive of God willing or needing to be present in her in a more obvious way, least of all in a way that would encourage her to go within herself in some final sense to commune with God. On the contrary, she insists that for God to be known we must enter into communion with others in and through whom God is known. This is her understanding both of the need for true worship and of the nature of the true Church.

We observe that the trouble with what she says is that we can never be sure whether the words we are hearing and the actions we are witnessing are performed in her own strength and on her own authority or with the sanction, the strength and the authority of God. She laughs, and asks why it matters to us to be able to make such a distinction. But then she grows serious: we have betrayed a concern to find God in a way divorced from the way we live our lives, and therefore in a way that is fundamentally designed to allow us to know and experience God without those lives changing. For her, experience of God, knowledge of God, and living her own life – realizing her own being, her own deepest self – are not separable and cannot be. Not only is she not interested in learning how to perform such a separation; she vehemently refuses to try. She acknowledges that what she really means – which is to say and to risk a lot – is that to become someone through whom God can be known we must each in some sense become indistinguishable from God. Or at least, to put it more precisely, that if God is to be known in us, it will be through a process in which it has ceased to be possible (or desirable) to distinguish that which is of God from that which is of ourselves.

We express anxiety about this: doesn't it run the risk of a colossal pride in which we begin to make ourselves into God? This, she says, is completely to misunderstand the point and in fact to compound the error, for it is the kind of objection that someone will only make who does not understand it (rather like the argument Paul ridicules in Romans: 'let us go on sinning, so that grace may increase'; no one who has any sense of divine grace would use it). She points to Jesus, and explains that it is perfectly possible to take his self-description as Son of God in just this sense, but without inferring that he is claiming for himself the kind of importance that we lesser mortals would hanker after were we to make the same claim. It is possible, in fact, she argues, to see this self-description just as a natural piece of self-expression: for Jesus to describe himself otherwise would be for him to lie about himself and to mislead those who knew him. She does not and could not make a similar claim because it just would not be true of her self-understanding to make her identification with God so complete and total; she would equally be appalled if others insisted on attributing to her that kind of divine presence. And so we ask her who she is, and she for once gives us a straight answer (borrowing words ascribed to God, see Exodus 3.14), that could in a different mouth sound like blasphemy or pride but in her is born of the utmost humility: 'I am what I am, and I will be what I will be.'

THE INSIDE STORY

When the heroine of this tale contemplates her own life, and asks herself what ambitions she has to fulfil and what means she can employ to fulfil them, the question of her own introspective experience of God will not weigh heavily on her mind. She will realize that to whatever extent God is present within her, that presence is not there solely for her own benefit and will remain inaccessible unless she throws it into communicable form by voicing words and performing actions through which it can be known.

Her life story as perceived from outside will accordingly be a greater or lesser manifestation of God's presence, but her own sense of the presence of God will also depend upon these words and actions. She will not expect God to be present to her in a way she can grasp consciously, and so be aware of, other than through the same kinds of words and actions that she uses to communicate with others. Some of these words may only be thoughts inside her head that she does not voice publicly, but they will still be words, and like all words they will depend upon a vast field of meanings embodied in her culture, inculcated by her tradition, and as such dependent on other people.

Words and actions will therefore reflect back to her the presence of God which is perceived in her by others, but the same restrictions will remain: she will be unable to distinguish knowledge of God from knowledge of self, for the manifestations of both will irrupt from the chaos below thought in an indistinguishable jumble. Like all human beings, except the Jesus of the Christian faith, she will be aware of a gulf between the self she is and the self she could be, and to some extent she will understand that gulf as the product of her failure to incorporate the fruits of God's deep presence in her life, but that will only drive her to more strenuous self-communication and inter-personal communion in pursuit of a greater awareness and realization of her self.

The effect of all this will be that self-fulfilment and self-knowledge will cease to be distinguishable from responding to God's call and knowing God: she will say and do what as a matter of fact she judges it best to say and do. She will interpret 'best', if we ask her, in terms of pursuit of those paths which resonate most deeply within her, rather like a mouse running a maze which tries different routes until it finds one that works, or someone blowing over a bottle, altering the force of the breath until it evokes a resonant echo governed by the geometry of the bottle.

Many obvious objections will occur to her: can it really be right to pursue apparently so selfish a path defined only by her own conviction? But she knows that the one thing introspection and dwelling on her own words and actions tell her is what she feels most deeply drawn to and what she shies away from. These resonances will neither be ignored nor denied: she must either be this, which is to say that she will pursue the course dictated by her own sense of her deepest self, or she will be nothing; she will have betrayed herself. And in betraying herself she will also have betrayed everyone who knows her (just as they, in betraying themselves, betray her), everyone for whom she must be what she is and what she will be.

What of the possibility, even the high probability, that she will take a wrong turn; and what of the dangers attendant upon listening only to herself? The possibility of error is intrinsic to life, and in exploring the essentially uncharted space of our own lives we must of necessity make decisions on the basis of seemingly inadequate evidence, being subsequently bound by the consequences. She does not and cannot listen only to herself: by virtue of the fact that God's presence can only be manifested and rendered accessible through words and actions whose meanings are derived from their place in a community, a tradition, a culture, that culture is inevitably and inescapably involved in her self-examination. If the culture is completely wrong, it will not supply the linguistic and other tools that she needs to reach the deeper levels of her self. (The words of Psalm 139, quoted earlier, put her in touch with aspects of her self she could not perhaps reach without those words.) In other words, just as is the case with worship, Scripture, doctrine and prayer, she must – if she is to be that self which God has made her, and therefore that self whom God would have her be – seek out the ways of knowing and obeying God which enable her to resonate with the deepest parts of her being. And those resources may require her to step outside the boundaries of her tradition and her culture (just as Jesus stepped outside the boundaries of what many deemed acceptable behaviour in order to find and to fulfil his own vocation).

Since she is prohibited by her own deepest convictions from rejecting the company of others, they will be for her, as she observes their lives from outside, just as much a guide and inspiration, potentially just as much living embodiments of God's presence in their lives as her own words and actions are living embodiments of God's presence in her self. She will remind herself of Dietrich Bonhoeffer's twofold injunction: let she who is afraid of being alone beware of community; let she who is afraid of community beware of being alone (*Life Together*). But that said, she will not attempt to side-step her own final responsibility for her own life, and nothing others say and do can take that responsibility away. In the end, she must decide what she must do. That for most human beings such decisions involve repeated error will not dissuade her from making decisions; Jesus was not in a different position, and no doubt received both inspiration and erroneous counsel from those he knew ('Get behind me, Satan!' Mark 8.33). What her reflection upon the life of Jesus tells her most forcefully is that it is simply inconceivable that we should need both to seek for those paths that lead to the deepest resonances with self and other and world, and then be required to look elsewhere in order to find God. If God is not accessible in her deepest self, then God is – in any sense that can possibly make any difference to her life – nowhere.

But perhaps the strongest instinct she has is that she should also trust her doubts as manifestations of the inner presence, as dissonant clues to the contradictions in and barriers to a worthwhile life. She cannot understand, for example, what role a mediating priesthood can have in the presence of an 'intrascendent' God. She is baffled by what purpose worship serves when God's service is wholly fulfilled in realizing her own life. she cannot and frankly will not accept doctrinal formulations that are supposed to contribute to her 'salvation' which she finds it impossible to incorporate into her world-view. And she has so great a sense of the sovereign love of God that she feels no need to protect him against her own (or anyone else's) sceptical questioning. The complete freedom she feels in God enables her to be entirely herself, to follow her own life, to ask her own questions, to reject (or put on 'hold' for later consideration) those things she finds meaningless and unintelligible.

She is aware that in some hands such a faith would licence self-delusion, but she does not regard the possibility of abuse as a good reason for rejecting a right path. After all, she reasons, God took exactly that risk in making the world. She is not complacent; she does not believe that if she does nothing, God will do everything. She accepts instead that her decisions will shape her destiny. Her vocation lies in throwing her own sense of freedom in God into communicable form in the hope that others will find it possible to live their lives in the same freedom. This is her creed, her hope, her worship, her prayer and the means of her discipleship: 'I am what I am, and I will be what I will be.'

THE UNTOLD STORY

It is clear that a great deal can and does go wrong with our development as human beings, and that our ability to sense the presence of God may be great, small or negligible. Sometimes our dissatisfaction with our lives is apparent to those who observe us from outside through our worried faces, depression, and words and actions that betray inner conflict. Sometimes others may perceive us as fulfilled and content, the kind of person many would envy and be ready to change places with, while inside we are conscious of greater or lesser conflicts between what we are and what we feel we would be were we able to bring our deep self into the open, to communicate it more fully for the benefit of ourselves and others, and so to accentuate its influence on the way we live our lives.

To whatever extent our heroine suffers from these pangs of dissatisfaction, she is faced with a choice. One option is to press ahead regardless, to bring her deepest self into the open by throwing it into a communicable form and hence enabling internal and external resonances to be set up as it echoes in her own consciousness and others' experiences of her. The alternative is to suppress her deepest self and employ impersonal and ready-made masks or roles that do not require investment of her self and can as such both absorb and deflect criticism or hurt that is levelled against her.

The price she pays for this subterfuge is to lose touch with her self, or at least to diminish her sense of self; the price others pay is that they are denied the genuine experience of human depth that can only come from her free self-expression. Rather than encounter, or be suspended over, a well of infinite potentiality, she and they are instead suspended over a bottomless void that is filled with alien sounds.

If she adopts such a strategy – and there are many good and persuasive reasons for her to do so – she will justify it by believing that she is finding a way to survive in a hostile environment. The trouble is that, understandable as that may be, what she is preserving is a self that cannot grow and change, a self that is fossilized in its inner sanctum, perhaps communing with an intrascendent God, but never able to move forward or upward out of that state.

Erica Berman, the social psychologist, once described what she perceives as one of the most pressing problems of our age as 'a scarcity of opportunities to be someone' (in Parker and Shotter, *Deconstructing Social Psychology*, p. 4); what she meant is that we live in an age which offers us countless masks, countless ready-made roles that we can play in order to disguise our deepest selves, but few opportunities to express ourselves as we really are (which will led us to become more than we are already). The helpful suggestions that deserve a retort such as, 'Get thee behind me, Satan!' are those which tempt us to settle for less than we are capable of being in order to live 'a quiet life'. But the cost and the sacrifice of such a strategy are almost infinite, for we lose touch with our deepest selves the more infrequently we give expression and utterance to them, and the fewer our opportunities to be someone, the less we have a sense of the someone we can be. This is the deep sense in which, 'What good will it be for a woman if she gains the whole world, yet forfeits her soul?' (see Matthew 16.26, adapted), must be understood.

Part of her conflict, of course, is that she perceives a contradiction between her self-expression and her obligations. She may have a career, children, a husband, relatives, social standing, each of which draw her in different directions, each of which require her to be someone they need her to be rather than the self she truly is. And what she finds difficult to act upon – what we all find difficult to act upon – is the conviction that in failing to be the self she truly is, the unique deep self that she can realize in her self-communication, far from fulfilling her responsibilities, she is reneging on them, betraying those whom she loves as surely as she is betraying her self. For, as she knows, most of those who do act on this conviction do so in a way that trivializes or prostitutes it, for what they imagine to be their realization of a deep self through their appropriation of an opportunity to be someone is really no more than a striving after the attainment of another kind of ready-made mask (wealth, power, fame, influence).

In her own life she is deeply troubled by such conflicts, by the difficulty of deciding whether an unfulfilled ambition arises from and is a betrayal of a feature of her deep self, or whether it is just another empty lifestyle that she does well to ignore. She is acutely conscious of the problem of distinguishing between words and actions that communicate something of her deep self and words and actions that defend and protect her from harm.

The problem is compounded once she realizes that her friends and her society are not always reliable guides when it comes to deciding what she should do. Their ambitions for her may seek to make her a pawn in their own elaborate games by preventing her from voicing convictions they find unsettling or performing actions they find distasteful. Their injunctions may as easily be invitations to betray herself as the wise counsel of perceptive friends concerned to enable her to bring her self into full bloom. Sometimes even a suggestion that she should relinquish a responsibility she feels greatly in order to satisfy her own needs is ambiguous: is she being invited to reinforce or invent a pattern of behaviour that someone else wishes to see introduced into society; or is the path set before her likely to produce a genuine increase in her self-understanding and a corresponding increase in the richness of their lives?

She is aware that to allow resonance to take the full strain of this vast set of difficulties may be to hang too much upon it, but she also knows that resonance is a fitting metaphor for something that emanates from oneself, and sounds in a space far greater than one could otherwise hope to fill. The way she thinks of it, her eyes cannot fill a theatre, but her voice can, and what her spoken words and deliberate actions can evoke that sight cannot, is an immediate and authentic response from the space upon which they fall and into which they enter. Unlike reason and vision, sound can embrace multi-dimensional realities and not only can be but must be configured and constrained by the diverse features of the world in which it resounds. All the features of her life that need to be taken into consideration can be embodied in this experience of resonance: her career, her children, her husband, her faith, her true and deepest self. What she has to do – arguably all she has to do – is to discover what sounds to make, what questions to ask, and how best to attune herself to the resonant echoes that those questions will evoke as they fall upon the depths of reality.

Moses asked whom he should say had sent him. And he heard the answer: 'I am who I am, and I will be what I will be.'

A FANTASTIC STORY

The distinction between the outside-in and the inside-out can be illustrated from one particular reading of human ambition, and therefore from the relationship between what I am and what I may one day be.

Suppose, to take an everyday example, that there is a particular motor car that we yearn to own. It need not be very grand: for most of us ambition should be credible rather than fantastic; a smart new Ford may be a more realizable goal than a smart new Rolls-Royce. As we go about our business we notice others driving the car of our dreams; we admire and envy and perhaps even respect them: they have achieved what we would like to achieve. We forget, for the time being, that they too have their dreams, that their ambitions lead them to yearn for those things which lie beyond our wildest imagining.

This process involves a confusion of the outside-in with the inside-out: we imagine that to be the person we admire, respect or envy from-outside-in would be to enjoy a sense of self-esteem coloured by exactly those feelings of admiration, respect and envy. I imagine that 'if I were you' I would feel about myself the way I feel about you. This is an illusion. Because we should be content with the admiration we bestow on them from-outside-in, we imagine that they must enjoy self-esteem and contentment from-inside-out. Because we respect from-outside-in, we imagine self-respect from-inside-out. Yet the purchase of a new motor car illustrates this fallacy rather well: the motor car only looks good, large, impressive and desirable while we are looking from the outside; once inside, cars are much the same, and they all afford much the same view.

Louise has experienced this in the way men 'read' the way she dresses. Men, she has found, tend to think that she dresses well (and she dresses very well) to please and attract them. They are usually dumbfounded when she explains to some would-be suitor that, on the contrary, she dresses well to please herself. Her clothes are not worn to encourage others to think of her as she is not; they are worn to tell others and herself what she is.

A gnawing doubt which lies deep within many of us shows itself in our inability to feel accepted for what we are, warts and all. It leads us to try or to yearn to be something or someone that we are not. And only when we are completely at one with ourselves can we hope to offer others praise, applause and adulation that is genuine: no human being can overflow who is not first brim full.

And I suspect that deep down there is in each of us a fear that we may not actually be good enough, that to be known for what we really are will lead to our rejection, and that rejection by the other is always more valid than affirmation by the self. And so we live illusory, fantastic lives, fabricated from the left-overs of passing expressions of disapproval by those who neither know us nor care to know us, but who leave their scars, their 'I do not approve of you.'

And ultimately, belief in God must have something to do with experiencing a love that gives us permission to give ourselves permission to love ourselves, learning to mean what we say when we reply to the Great Question, 'Who are you?' with: 'I am who I am, and I will be what I will be.'

Why does a single phrase refuse to move from its central place in our heroine's mind? Why is that phrase Erica Berman's 'scarcity of opportunities to be someone'? Because in her heart of hearts, she knows that she is someone and yet that the world somehow conspires to prevent her from being that self she truly is.

And she feels this most acutely in her religious life, where her experience of the Church is of a body that always wants her to be someone she is not, someone who does things she does not want to do, who believes things she cannot believe, and who claims to know things she does not know.

She feels that her life – like so many lives (she is not fool enough to think herself alone in this respect) – has not just been given over to servicing the requirements of other lives (husband, children, parents, work-mates, friends), for that too would and should be construed just as self-pity based upon a reluctance to do her communal duty. No, her sorrow is far greater than this: she feels that in sacrificing herself to their needs she has actually betrayed them, the husband, children, parents, work-mates and friends that she loves *by failing to make real her own true self*. She has taken the easy way that involves being what they want her to be (and have made her) rather than that self she knows that she can be (knows better than they) and that could, in being itself, *make them*. Hers has become a betrayal not only of herself, but of those whom she loves as well. Allowing them to make her less than she is, she has made them less than they could be. And in realizing that she experiences the deepest sorrow, for in her weakness she has betrayed everything.

And therefore, briefly, finally, and painfully, she knows her name not as a name of glory, but as a name of sorrow and condemnation, for her name has become itself in its clarity and precision her condemnation, a token of all that she has betrayed: 'I am what I am, and I will be what I will be.'

From the depths of the despair occasioned by this realization, Louise is reborn in the light of one pure and simple thought: that any power on earth that tries to make her into something she is not is a corrupt power, and worthy neither of her obedience nor her respect. She knows, however, that in weakness, fear, and concern for those she loves, she may nonetheless succumb to the world's intimidations. But she also knows that there will always remain a light in her heart that has not been extinguished by them, the product of a living flame. And so, come what may, she is reborn in the image of the God in whose presence alone she is most fully that self she truly is: 'I am what I am, and I will be what I will be.'

What about Christianity?

Christianity is fundamentally about death and resurrection, and so is this book. In one, minor, sense it is about the death and resurrection of one particular Christian and that particular Christian's faith. To that extent is it intensely personal, at times almost outrageously so. No doubt it is also sometimes mildly – I hope only mildly – offensive inasmuch as it dares to challenge some cherished beliefs and assumptions. But even in this very personal, particular way it is a testament to the faith beyond faith that allows even faith to question itself, that allows even faith to face its own death, and to dare to utter the cry of dereliction, 'My God, my God, why have you forsaken me?' (Matthew 27.46, etc.).

This sense of a faith that enables even faith to doubt, to question and to die, is something which is almost too personal to write about. It is the journey through the death of a faith based upon fear and superstition and external authority and a kind of endowment insurance view of religion in which, when we die, we receive both reversionary and terminal bonuses.

This journey is a death that cannot be undertaken without a sense of the presence of the God who never leaves us alone.

And if there is a resurrection in any life, most of all mine, it must in the end be a work of God. When faith finds itself led into the grave, brought low by the injustices and cruelties of the world, worn down by cares and led to or beyond the brink of despair, it must in the end abandon itself to God. This was true even for Jesus, that a faith capable of moving mountains, calming storms and raising the dead had finally to succumb to the power of death.

And I think that only those who have been to this lowest ebb of life's great tide can truly understand what it is to pray in the wonderful words of the Book of Common Prayer, 'seeing that we have no power of ourselves to help ourselves'. Of course it is not fashionable these days to confess such utter helplessness. Humankind has raised itself up as an idol capable of solving all its own problems. But Christianity teaches us something very different, and that teaching is at its roots about death and resurrection. Between the two, and that which turns the one into the other, is nothing but the power of the love of God. To fail to see this is to fail to see anything. This is the fundamental claim which Christianity makes: the Word spoken in and by Jesus made the universe; the Word spoken in and by Jesus entered into life in the universe in the fullest possible sense; the Word spoken in and by Jesus loves the universe and everything in it; the Word spoken in and by Jesus is spoken to you and to me, whom that same Word uttered by the one true God loves as his own children and friends.

This is what Christianity is about.